CW00507421

Coach yourself with a Pen

Journaling exercises to get you out of your head and into your life

Claire Pearce

Published June 2023

Cover adapted from design by Fatih Kaya on Canva

DEDICATION

This book is dedicated to my fellow journalers and writers who join me in writing and exploring. You amaze and inspire me with your beautiful, messy and vulnerable words.

CONTENTS

1	Introduction	Pg 1
2	Chapters	Pg 8
3	Journaling	Pg 12
4	Coaching	Pg 18
5	Knowing what you want	Pg 23
6	It's all about you	Pg 25
7	Other people	Pg 28
8	What to do with what you surface	Pg 31
9	The Exercises	Pg 35

Life Manifesto — Pg 39

Hostile or friendly Universe — Pg 40
What do you expect? — Pg 43
What do you believe? — Pg 46
What do you deserve? — Pg 49
Whose agenda are you on? — Pg 52
Definition of success — Pg 55
Permission — Pg 60
Thank you (gratitude) — Pg 62

Warming up — Pg 66

Brain dump — Pg 67
Six senses — Pg 70
Bible dip — Pg 73

GROW

Reality - What's happening now — Pg 76

Into the weeds — Pg 77
From the mountain top — Pg 80
Newspaper article — Pg 83

Goals - Exploring	Pg 86
If I lived forever	Pg 87
Alternative lives	Pg 90
Wouldn't it be lovely?	Pg 93
Goal - Clarifying	Pg 96
Explain yourself	Pg 97
Manifest memoir	Pg 100
30 Words	Pg 103
Options – What you could do	Pg 106
The last thing I'd do	Pg 108
The last time I …	Pg 111
What does the radiator think?	Pg 114
What's Next? – What you will do	Pg 118
Planning and mitigating	Pg 121
Taking action	Pg 125
Reviewing, reflecting and learning	Pg 127
Enjoyed, Noticed, Learned	Pg 128
Examples	Pg 133
10 Resources	Pg 156
References	Pg 160
Thank you	Pg 161
About Me	Pg 162

1. INTRODUCTION

Hi, I'm Claire and I want you to have an easier and more enjoyable life. A life where you feel fulfilled and satisfied, even happy. I want you to know that you can make a difference to your life and that you have inner resources just itching to come out and help you.

I want you to feel inspired to help yourself, and that includes knowing when to ask for help from others. That's why I wrote this book, so that you can help yourself to do all of this and have the life you want.

Being happy is rarely about acquiring 'stuff' or achieving big shiny new goals and I've found that most people just need to take a breath and come back to themselves to get what they need and remember what they want.

It's not what we want to hear of course. We all want big changes and magic answers.

But it's the small adjustments to your life that generally do the trick. Changes that help you to reconnect with yourself, to do the things you enjoy, to remember that, even when it doesn't feel like it, you have a choice, you are good enough, and that you deserve the things you want.

I'm here to help you learn easy to use tools that are great for reflecting and learning, self-discovery, achieving goals and solving problems.

You can use them on your own or with other people.

Best of all, you can use these tools 24/7 which makes them great for 'in the moment' challenges.

I discovered creative journaling at a weekend workshop in around 2016, five years after I trained as a coach and it transformed my life, saved it even.

Firstly, as an outlet for all the stuff* that didn't have anywhere to go, then, as a way to get to know and understand myself. To bring out inner courage, wisdom and creativity I didn't know I had, and ultimately, to make life easier and more enjoyable. As I say, this is what I want for you too.

After that first workshop I attended, I had the journaling bug, especially journaling with other people.

I wrote with everyone who couldn't think of an excuse not to quickly enough, and after I'd run out of people I knew, I started running groups to find new people to write with.

Since then, I've run hundreds of workshops and courses privately and for organisations.

I've created all the exercises in this book but some were naturally inspired by and adapted from other exercises I've picked up along the way. I've mentioned in the resources the courses I've attended and any books I particularly recommend.

*Stuff - By 'stuff' I just mean unexpressed emotions; frustration, anger, regret, and more. Generally, the stuff we consider more 'negative.'

Don't take my word for it

Here are just a few testimonials (more can be found at clairepearce.uk/what people say) on the benefits of journaling and free-writing:

"I discovered the incredible benefits of journaling in my daily life. Not only did it help me organise my thoughts and clarify my goals, but it also gave me a better understanding of my emotions and behaviours. By writing down my thoughts, I was able to reflect on my experiences and learn valuable lessons." CG

"I forgot to mention last week that a new tool I've been using in last three months, inspired by the coaching sessions has been, download writing. When I've had something on my mind, going round and round, and round again, usually in the early hours, I've been picking my phone notepad and typing until the thoughts are more processed or downloaded. (Low brightness settings of course). It's been great for better thinking, self-coaching through something, peace of mind and going back to sleep. There's also some trace of thoughts, ideas, even actions to refer to the next morning. Can't tell you how powerful that has been for me. I'm a fan, thank you. BC

I have now learned how to make this (journaling) a part of my daily life, the benefits of which are amazing. GC

A complete novice to free writing (verging on sceptic). I could never have imagined the value to be gained from putting pen to paper and just letting your hand move - the pen taking you in whatever direction it saw fit. I gained invaluable headspace that allowed me to take stock of my reality and the challenges it entails. I reassessed the expectations I placed on myself, took a step back and started to learn the invaluable art of delegation. I finally had some space to start pushing boundaries and taking risks, which was both exciting and effective." WB

"I was able to make some clarity in what was really bothering me at that stage and learned about free flow writing which is something I have kept using ever since." MM

"A complete novice to free writing (verging on sceptic), I could never have imagined the value to be gained from putting pen to paper and just letting your hand move - the pen taking you in whatever direction it saw fit." WR

"Love how free-writing can be such fun but also uncover some interesting/deep stuff!" HF

"I was cynical about how useful writing could be, but when I read back what I'd written and selected the words that jumped out at me I understood how helpful it was. It made me look at things in a different way. It was beneficial in the way talking to a counsellor is; that you're getting input from another person & I'm looking at things in different ways which I would/could never do on my own. It felt good to be understood without judgment. I get a sense of well-being when I discover new things about myself. KP

"Coach Yourself with a Pen (the Course) unlocked some quite profound revelations for me about what was going on inside my head and helped me identify some practical actions I could take to address a particular issue. AP

"Thank you for introducing me to the transformative art of writing. I feel like I have reconnected to parts of myself that I have forgotten about." AV
"... I began to explore writing freely in my own time, especially journaling which helped me release a lot of the blocks I was experiencing in other parts of my life." VR

In an exercise I call, 'What does the radiator think?' (Featured in the exercises) I had participants write from an item they felt represented creativity for them and to have that object tell them the 'secret of creativity.' Here's what SP wrote from her pen: "My pen says the secret of creativity is being open at all times to the possibility of creativity. Stop boxing yourself *in. You don't need a specific time, a specific book, a specific pen, in order to create. You can create any time wherever you are. You don't - shouldn't - think, 'I have the wrong book with me,' or 'I should be doing this, or this...now isn't the right time.' Why isn't it? Why does it come bottom of the list after everything else? Jobs to do will always be there, and you will never run out. If you wait until they're done, you will never get the chance. So if there is an itch to be scratched, drop the other stuff and scratch it. 'Creativity is a dog. If you don't feed it, it will tear your house apart.' Think on this. And act on it. Who cares (apart from you) if stuff doesn't get done? If it means you birth something instead?"*

"The exercise left me feeling grounded. In doing it I finally recognised my ability for creativity. I discovered a richness to my inner world that delighted me and made me want to explore further. I never knew I could create my own world in my imagination." NB

This book is

This book is your new best friend, available 24/7 to help you at the very least, get out the things that may be swirling around in your head, going nowhere.

It's here to help you if you want:

- A way to create headspace and declutter your mind
- Tools to help you define and achieve what you want
- To explore and discover who you really are
- A way to offload and manage stress, worry and anxiety
- A way to externalise and reflect on experiences and feelings
- To expand your thinking and imagine a different future
- A way to keep motivated and stay focused
- To build more journaling into your life
- To tap into your creativity

I'll help you by giving you tools you can use 24/7 to:

- Make sense of experiences and the world around you
- Externalise your internal landscape and unleash inner resources
- Get new insights and perspectives
- Build your creative confidence
- Build a better relationship with yourself

This book isn't

This book isn't a formula for success, offering you a particular kind of lifestyle to aspire to. We're all different and need to live our own lives. In addition, I can't tell you exactly what worked for me and when.

Insights, shifts, realisations, revelations are made up of a whole range of conversations, information, experiences and all happen on their own schedule - rarely when we're looking and rarely at the moment, we'd like them to. As I like to say: *Change happens on a Tuesday afternoon when no-one's looking.*

All that said, I do know, with certainty, that journaling has been a significant help to me along the way and that's why I get a bit preachy about it.

My story is far from linear, and thankfully, far from over. I promise you I'm as flawed as I ever was, but I'm happier about who I am and how I live my life, and for me, that's success.

Finally, this book isn't meant to replace meaningful one to one work, coaching or otherwise. There is a great deal to be gained by using creative journaling alongside your coaching or therapeutic journey, it was definitely helpful for me. Here though, it's simply a way to deal with problems and challenges in the moment and give you a stronger sense of agency.

2. CHAPTERS

Journaling

A brief introduction to how journaling can help and how you can use it to coach yourself and get to know yourself.

- Journaling
- Free-writing
- Creativity
- Materials
- General journaling tips

Coaching

A brief introduction to coaching and it's aims. I'll talk about the principles and how you can coach yourself.

- Coaching
- Coaching yourself
- Talking to yourself (dialoguing)
- Basic GROW Model

Knowing what you want

A little on knowing and not knowing what you want and how to deal with that.

- You don't have to know what you want
- Themes
- When you do know what you want

It's all about you

An important chapter on the importance of your relationship with yourself and how to look after yourself.

- Your relationship with yourself
- Looking after yourself

Other people

Even though this book is about coaching yourself, you'll probably still need other people for support or some additional external perspective and this chapter talks about how best to do that.

- Working with someone else
- Guidance for working with someone else
- Asking for feedback/ideas

What to do with what you surface

Here I've outlined my favourite techniques to help you deal with what you surface, in addition to the reflection questions that go with each exercise.

- Check and choose
- Reframing
- Learned Optimism
- Change your questions

The Exercises and a final Pep Talk

I've given you exercises that follow the flow of the basic coaching model GROW. Each one has a brief introduction and instructions for you to write and questions to help you reflect on what you've surfaced. I've also included a brief word to encourage and inspire you to get stuck in and do things your way.

- Guidance
- Free-writing rules
- Lists
- Reviewing
- General reflection questions
- A final Pen Talk

The Exercises

- Life Manifesto
- Warming up
- Reality - What's happening now
- Goals: Exploring and Clarifying
- Options – What you could do
- What's next? – What you will do
- Planning and mitigating
- Taking action
- Reviewing, reflecting and learning

Examples

I've listed my initial responses to each prompt here, at the back of the book as I know some of you will feel happier seeing a brief example. Ideally though, I want you to write as freely as possible without influence from me.

Resources

Books and TED talks are listed here as well as help that is available should you need it.

3. JOURNALING

Often, just writing down your thoughts about something can be enough to make you go, "Oh yes, the answer is obvious!"

There's something about seeing your internal landscape externalised onto the page before you. It's just so very powerful.

Journaling helps you to make sense of what you're experiencing and the world around you. You don't have to have any interest in, or experience of writing and all the rules are thrown out when it comes to journaling. You don't have to use grammar, spelling or even make any sense; you can be truly free on the page.

Try it now. Stop what you're doing and write for a few minutes on the topic of journaling. What's your experience? If you've never journaled, what are you worried about? Whatever comes, just keep writing or a few minutes.

Writing and journaling are good for you mentally *and* physically, and there is plenty of research to back this up.

One of the most useful benefits is that you get fresh new perspectives which are so hard to come by when it's just you and your thoughts swirling around in your head.

When it comes to things you want to achieve, journaling packs a real punch and turns thoughts into tangible intentions.

And as if these aren't good enough reasons, you can use journaling 24/7, for example, when your brain is spinning in the middle of the night; to reflect, to make decisions, to ease anxiety and stress, and so much more.

Free-writing

Most of the exercises will require you to use free-writing rules. The idea is that you don't think too much and let your pen run free on the page. You may know about this as free-flow, non-stop, stream-of-consciousness or wild writing.

With free-writing, you:

- Stick a timer on, generally for five minutes
- Don't stop writing – don't think – keep your pen moving
- Go where your pen goes, even if it's off topic
- Look after yourself if you surface emotions by either writing into the detail and describing it (which can be self-soothing), or come back to it when it feels like a better time
- Are kind to yourself and don't judge what you write - this is a tool to get thoughts on the page, you're not writing to produce a 'thing.'

If you'd like to give free-writing a go now, follow the instructions above and write from the prompt: 'Freedom means…'

I'll get onto reviewing and reflecting in the exercises that follow, but in the meantime, as well as reading back what you've written, if you can, read it out loud for even more insight – I've noticed completely different things in what I've written when I've done this, either to myself or someone else.

Creativity

I believe everyone is creative and that you just need to find your own particular way of expressing it. You may or may not have found yours yet, but whether or not writing is your thing, these methods will likely stir your creative juices.

If writing is your thing, you may find it rekindles the poems you used to write, the story you want to tell, the journaling you used to find so rewarding.

So, get ready to be inspired.

Materials

It may sound like a silly thing to cover, but it's something I'm often asked about.

Whilst there is research to say writing by hand is better; it helps us to remember and be more honest for example, my answer is always, "if it gets you writing, it's in."

When I had my corporate job, I sometimes had a couple of minutes on my computer just venting and it was extremely therapeutic. Using my computer in that situation made it easy for me to do a bit of journaling when I needed it, which was often.

I also used to have a fold-out keyboard that I used to balance on my knee on the bus when I lived in London. I could type away - without seeing my phone screen - and just get 'it' all out.

Sometimes I re-read what I wrote, sometimes I didn't. Ideally though, I like to write in a notebook, as much as anything, because it gives me some screen-free time.

As for notebooks, the best advice I can give is to start with something 'scrappy.' I used to have a pack of 'five for a pound' skinny exercise books which gave me permission to write anything I liked.

There's nothing more certain to stop you journaling than a 'beautiful' notebook. I have some beautiful notebooks that I still can't bring myself to write in and that's fine.

I generally go for Moleskins now because I like the paper and the soft cover, and the size. If you must have a beautiful one, make sure you have scrappy ones too to actually do some journaling in.

My pen of choice is a Papermate Flair. I'm not on commission but I should be as I tell anyone who will listen to try them and go through a large number of them myself.

They come in lovely colours but most importantly, they're easy on the hand. A biro takes its toll after about half a page whereas a more felt-tippy nib glides a bit easier.

General journaling tips

In case you've never journaled and would like a few pointers to get you started, here are some of my top tips:

What to write

- It's worth thinking about your journaling goals. Do you want to get to know yourself better, capture what you've done, express gratitude, capture dreams?
- *Allow yourself to be positive - journaling isn't just for problems. Allow yourself to be mundane - often the little simple things lead to more interesting insights.*

How much to write

- Set yourself up for success. If you think you'll write for half an hour a day, set a goal of 10 minutes instead. This leaves you wanting more but also, if you get into it, there's nothing to stop you carrying on.
- *Allow yourself to write only one word if that's all you feel like.*

Where to do it

- Don't get caught up in the fantasy of the perfect chair, with the perfect view, the perfect cosy shawl and notebook etc. If you grab five minutes in the kitchen whilst making your breakfast, so be it.
- *Allow yourself time to try out different places, be open minded.*

Confidentiality

- Write over other words – get a cheap novel from a charity shop and just write over it which disguises what you've written.
- Lock it away or destroy it once you've got what you need.
- *Allow yourself to be as protective/sensitive as you need – not what you think is acceptable.*

Most important of all, there are no journaling police. If there were, I would have been arrested several times over.

Finding a time, place and way to journal that works for you is the most important thing.

4. COACHING

Coaching gives you the space you need to find your own answers, even if that's that you need more information/help. No-one knows what you need better than you, or how best to go about getting the things you want.

So, beware of advice; it's normally driven by what the advice-giver would do, which is probably well-meaning but not always helpful to you. Even if the advice is good, research shows that you're much more likely to take action if you've uncovered the next step yourself rather than taking advice. This is at the heart of coaching.

In order to help you find your own answers a coach gives you space to take a breath, step back and see your situation with fresh eyes, surfacing new insights and perspectives. A coach will ask you questions to dig a bit deeper and help you find internal resources to help you move forward.

Coaching yourself

Coaching yourself using journaling works in a similar way. You're externalising the internal by writing (instead of talking) which means you can then talk to that part of yourself, on the page … Yes, I'm encouraging you to talk to yourself. In my opinion, not talking to yourself is actually where madness lies.

Dialoguing

Talking to yourself on the page is called dialoguing in the journaling world and you'll see it come up often in these exercises.

You'll also begin to notice things in your journaling that will catch your eye which you can then explore further. You'll become your own observer.

Coaching yourself means you have free, 24/7 access to resources that can help you right when you need it.

GROW Model

There are lots of coaching models, but for the sake of simplicity and the fact you've probably come across it before, I've used the GROW model as the basic structure for ordering the exercises.

GROW is simply:

Goal – What you want
Reality – What's happening now
Options – What you could do
What's Next? – What you will do

In the exercises, I've listed *Reality* before *Goal*. As I explain, I find it's more useful to explore what's making you want the thing you want as it can often influence the goal itself. But to explain the model I've laid it out here in order:

Goal – What do you want?

Coaching can act as either a way to discover what's in the way of doing what you want or getting clear on what it is you want. It's generally a bit of both from my experience. What you want can be as simple as an answer to a decision, a resolution to a conflict, right through to, 'what do I want to do with my life?'

I encourage you to spend more time exploring what it is you want before leaping into action. I realise this is annoyingly sensible and often frustrating. You want change to happen now. But I've learned that slowing down and really taking my time when I have an urge to rush is always the right thing to do. Also, you may find that what you want is actually different to what you originally thought.

Reality – What's happening now

We can get lost in our own heads in difficult situations or overwhelmed by what's happening/not happening. Small problems or obstacles can become an impenetrable 'whole' - something we can do nothing about because of x, y, or z.

Standing back and reviewing 'what's actually happening' will not only give you some perspective, but it can also help to reveal the facts. Have you really 'tried everything,' are you making assumptions about what other people think or know? It can also help you to see some alternative solutions.

At best, taking the time to stand back can reveal a chink in the armour of a situation. A question mark around something that you couldn't see before that you can explore and can lead to a way out. At the very least, you'll get a fresh look at what's going on, and just seeing it from a different angle shifts your energy.

Options - What you could do

This is where you explore everything that you could possibly do, including the impossible. It's the same principle as brainstorming; you get down as many things as you can. The more you come up with, the more ideas you'll get. These exercises will also show you ways to get additional perspectives and ideas without speaking to another soul.

Thomas Edison is famous for saying, "*When you have exhausted all possibilities, remember this – you haven't.*" I love this quote because it captures the essence of the idea of limitless possibilities. Whether you're at the beginning or end of a brainstorm, it's almost always true.

When you have your list, you then pick the option that feels best and go with that, remembering that you can change this. Holding outcomes lightly is one of the best things I've learned.

If something's not working, try something else.

What's next? What you will do

All this work is nothing without action. You have to do something in order to get things moving, even if it's something small and even if there's uncertainty. This can be a tricky place where fear and doubt can creep in, which is often what makes it hard to take action in the first place.

The *What's next?* should be a really small, absolutely do-able action, rather than setting yourself up for failure by setting expectations that are way too high.

Summary

This is – very roughly – how the GROW model works and honestly, if you think of something small right now and work through it at its very simplest, it can be really helpful, and quick.

It's my 'go to' for coaching myself. It's just so useful as a reminder to break things down and find a *What's next?*

I personally prefer to start with *Reality* and then focus on the *Goal*. It's my experience – and the experience of almost every other coach I know – that people often want something different and less dramatic to the thing they're certain they wanted at the start.

5. KNOWING WHAT YOU WANT

You don't have to know what you want

If you're someone who doesn't know what they want, firstly let me reassure you that a) it's hard to know and therefore it's OK, and, b) you are most definitely not alone. I've only come across about three people in my entire life who always knew what they wanted to be when they grew up. And finally, c) you probably do know but it's just so hidden under all the crapola that's built up through life that you can't access it. The good news is that journaling and clearing out the crapola will help you uncover your answers and there are some specific exercises to address this.

Themes

One thing that can help when you don't know exactly what you want is a theme, something I'm a big fan of. You may know that you want more love in your life, or you want to feel more connected to yourself, or that you want to be calmer. You don't have to know exactly how you're going to get these things at the outset but having a theme that captures the essence of what you want can help with day-to-day decisions. It can be a song, a word, an object, a question, anything that reminds you of what you want.

My most successful theme was simply, 'New.' I didn't know

what I wanted, but I knew for sure that I needed something new, so 'New' was my word; my theme. It informed what I did, decisions I made and more. In most cases, I would ask myself, "Is it new?" and if the answer was, "No" I did something different.

It was enough to loosen the soil around me and things changed, all leading me to where I am today – in a much happier and more satisfied place.

A theme opens you up to possibilities you may not consider. You can't fail with a theme and it by no means stops you from having goals if and when you want them.

I run a New Year theme workshop each January (followed by a quarterly check-in) to help you get to your theme. Go to clairepearce.uk for details.

When you do know what you want

It's great if you do know what you want, whether that's a change in career or a resolution to a conflict.

Sometimes though, in unpicking what you've decided you want, for example, 'a new job,' you may discover what you really want is connection or a deeper sense of satisfaction, which of course can come from several different outcomes, not just, 'getting a new job.'

So, it's always worth checking in on what the outcome you desire will give you and consider thinking about a theme too. It will help to harness your goal and keep you focused and motivated.

6. IT'S ALL ABOUT YOU

Your relationship with yourself

I've learned that my most important relationship is the one I have with myself. Journaling helped me to develop and strengthen that relationship by giving me a way to:

- Make sense of what happens (and what happened) in my life.

- Connect to what I feel. I needed to unclog myself of unprocessed emotions in order to get in touch with my feelings, to actually know how I feel.

- Find parts of myself I'd shoved away in a cupboard or had got stuck in the past. I talked to those parts of myself on the page. I comforted them, reclaimed them and became more whole, more myself. This is ongoing work and who knows, I may never find all the parts of me, but I've definitely got most of them now. If you'd like to read more about this, see my blog, *You can make you whole again*, available at clairepearce.uk/blog.

- Talk to the inner-critics (yes, there's more than one) who are just protecting more vulnerable parts of me. When I've given them space to say what they need and what they want me to know, they're very happy to be let off the hook from being on guard 24/7.

- Understand that negative messages I believed about myself were either just things someone said to me, or more subtly, an underlying message I received. As a child, in the moment we don't have the tools to challenge those messages or respond differently.

  For example, a punitive teacher calling you stupid or a parent telling you you're "a waste of space" may still be alive and well and bouncing around in your psyche. "I'm not good enough," is a classic that a lot of us either heard or felt. The great thing is that you can go back and challenge and question those things now, as the adult 'you.'

- Surface positive messages and aspects of myself that perhaps don't shout quite as loudly as the negative ones. All those voices are in there too; the nurturer, the carer, the encourager and inspirer. They live in our dazzlingly clever brains waiting to be called upon.

- Discover that the vulnerable/hidden parts of me (once fiercely guarded by the critics) contain wisdom, creativity and courage and actually help me, now, in the present.

If you've not experienced this kind of work before, I appreciate it may sound a little strange. I can say that it's not just my experience but that of others I've worked with.

Where these voices come from is not for me to say. I just know that they're there and that reclaiming them has been a rich and profound experience for me.

So, look at journaling as communicating with yourself; with all aspects of yourself, to build your most important relationship.

Looking after yourself

Looking after yourself is critical and it's where my desire to write this book came from - wanting to help you if you're alone, lost and don't know how to ask for help.

These tools may just have helped me in my darker days; to realise I had choices, to imagine something different, to simply get some relief.

Also, as my therapist used to say, "writing contains your feelings." It's been my experience that writing into and about my feelings, in detail, externalises them and the intensity often reduces.

There may be times though when you'll need the support of someone else. If you already have a therapist or coach, you may want to work through what comes up with them. Journaling alongside therapy/coaching etc., deepened 'the work' for me.

Luckily, if you don't have someone to hand and really need to talk, there are tons of interventions. As well as counsellors, coaches and therapists, there are football fields full of kind people wanting to listen and help for free, 24/7 - and I've listed some of the key ones at the end in the *Resources* section.

I eventually learned to ask for help, which was as much about an intention and an attitude as the actual act of asking. For me it was about being open and being OK with not having all the answers, something I struggled with for a long time.

7. OTHER PEOPLE

Working with someone else

Whether working with a professional or not, I'd always recommend doing this kind of journaling with someone else if you can — someone with the same good intentions as you.*

It could be a friend or a colleague. They may have the same goal as you, or not. The advantages of working with someone else are:

- It's a lovely shared experience and great for accountability
- You get to be heard (you can either read back what you wrote or just reflect on it).
- You get to witness someone else's internal landscape which can be just as enlightening as exploring your own.
- It becomes a more full-bodied experience. You think words, write them, read them, now you get to say them and hear them. This extra dimension often brings powerful insights.

A note on 'someone with the same good intention as you.' Not everyone finds it easy to know who that might be.

If that's you, this isn't always an easy one to navigate and may require some deeper work, but some guiding questions to ask yourself about someone you might choose are:

- *When you're with this person, how do you feel?*
- *After you've been with this person, how do you feel?*

If the answer isn't 'good' and 'good,' they're probably not the right person.

Again, this isn't an easy one to address in a paragraph, but hopefully these two questions will help.

Guidance for working with someone else

- Firstly, knowing you're going to share can affect what you write. Try to write for yourself first, you can then choose to leave out sections when it comes to sharing, or not share at all. It's more important that your pen - and you - are free.

- The first person can either read – word for word – what they've written, or just talk about what came up.

- When listening, and assuming the other person wants some kind of feedback (you can always just share and leave it at that) let the person finish before commenting. You can ask each other what kind of feedback you want, but the purpose of sharing in this context isn't about constructive feedback; was the writing good or bad, enjoyable or not, though of course there's no harm in mentioning you particularly enjoyed something.

  The listening and sharing are about being heard, witnessing the 'other' and sharing any insights or things you noticed, ideally without a judgement attached. E.g., "I noticed you slowed right down when you were talking about 'x'" Versus, "I think you're worried about 'x' because you slowed down." Let the other person hear what you noticed and come to their own conclusions. This is way more valuable.

- Once one person has shared, swap roles.

Asking for feedback/ideas

Whether you're working with someone or not, you can also just ask for some feedback on something specific, maybe around the different options that are open to you. We can be limited by our own experience and horizons. If you can be clear about your situation and your goal, it'll be really easy for others to throw in ideas.

Again, be careful who you choose. If someone has a vested interest in the course of action you take, it doesn't mean it's not valid, but bear that in mind.

For example, if a friend asked me about moving away, I may be at the mercy of my desire to keep them close and what I say may reflect that. Worse still, I may not realise that's what I'm doing.

We're all capable of this and that's why someone unconnected to your circumstances will give you more objective input.

8. WHAT TO DO WITH WHAT YOU SURFACE

It's important to read through what you've written, ideally out loud for extra insight (even if you're alone). Reflecting and digging into what you've written, or not written, and actually, how you've written (easy/hard/how you felt etc.) can lead to deep insights and of course, insights lead to change.

I've given you reflection questions for each exercise which will help you to reflect more deeply.

You may surface things that may be out of date and things that are not helping you, even if they did in the past. You may want to challenge beliefs, assumptions, generalisations etc. There are various ways to do this, some of them inherent in the exercises and reflection questions I've suggested.

Here are some additional ways to deal with things that will come up:

Check and choose your beliefs

You'll always hear coaches talking about 'limiting beliefs.' I prefer 'out of date beliefs,' for example, "I'm not creative," or "I'm silly and pointless." You can question these thoughts, these ingrained beliefs to see if you still think they're true.

31

You'll often find that on closer inspection experience has shown you that you're not silly and pointless, that you are creative, deserving, good enough etc. You can then decide to believe something different.

It's not always this simple, and other work may need to be done, but sometimes it really can be that simple. Review, check, make a new choice.

Reframing

Reframing is a beautifully simple thing. It's just about choosing where your focus goes, redirecting your attention to see another aspect of something.

Think about looking at a sculpture. You might stand in front of it and see one thing, then move around to the side and see something different. It's simply that, and of course, you get to choose the angle you prefer.

It can give you a sense of control and agency in your life and it can work for things in the past as well as the present. Here are two personal examples:

"I wasted years in my corporate career" has become, "Whilst there were bad parts of some of my roles in my corporate career, I actually learned a lot; about life and myself, and especially what I do/don't want. I also had fun which is really easy for me to forget."

"I'm a slow learner," has been reframed to: "I can be overly cautious with things I'm unsure about, but when I'm confident, I can be very quick to pick things up."

Learned optimism

Martin Seligman (one of the founders of positive psychology) wrote a book called *Learned Optimism*. It's essentially about reframing things on another level by seeing that they're not 'permanent,' 'pervasive' and 'personal.'

The book gives you tools to see things as 'temporary,' 'specific' and 'not personal,' which are obviously easier to overcome.

So, if you have a tendency to be more pessimistic than optimistic (and it's OK, it is what it is), I recommend giving the book a read.

I wrote a very brief summary of it in a blog called, *Pessimism and Mars Bars* which can be found at clairepearce.uk.

Change your questions

A great way to deal with feeling stuck about what you want or finding a solution to something is to change the question you're asking. I read a book a few years ago called, *Change your questions, change your life* by Marilee Adams. To be honest I found it a little hard work as the content is presented as a fable - my least favourite style.

But it tells you how good the content was behind the fable that I read on. I can honestly say that it really has changed my life. I have more freedom, more possibilities, more agency, more hope even. I'm always asking myself, "Am I asking the right question?"

Here's an example:

"What new job do I want?" could be asked as:

"How do I want to spend my time?" or

"What kind of life do I want?" or

"Who do I want to spend my time with?" (Something a very insightful colleague once asked me.)

So, when you're tackling something and you feel stuck, stop and ask yourself, "Can I ask a different question?" or "Am I asking the right question?" Have a little brainstorm and see what you can come up with, it can really open up new doors.

9. THE EXERCISES

So here we go, it's time to get into the exercises. Work through these methodically where it makes sense, otherwise, just pick an exercise that works for you and jump in. I've given three exercises in most of the sections. You only need to do one, whichever you prefer, but the more you do, the more insight you'll get.

We're all different and if you're someone who won't be comfortable unless you've seen an example or two, you can refer to the examples at the back of the book (page 133). But I'd really encourage you to start without being influenced by what I wrote, as I say, you cannot get this wrong, if you're writing something, you're doing the work.

Guidance

There are multiple exercises under each heading. One should be enough but the more you do, the more insights and perspective you'll get.

The following guidance will be repeated with each exercise:

Free-Writing Rules

- Set a timer for five minutes so you can let go into the journaling (you can always write more if you want to).
- Keep your pen moving (no editing or looking back) and follow your own emerging topic, even if it's about something else, it will still be important.
- If you get stuck, repeat the prompt or the last two words you wrote, if you feel resistance, annoyance or anything else, write about that.
- If you bump into difficult feelings, either write about them in detail (what does it feel like, where in your body can you feel it, what colour, texture, shape is it, etc.) or make a note to come back to it later when you have the support you need. Refer to the 'It's all about you' section for more.

Lists

In a list, you repeat the prompt each time followed by your response. It doesn't matter if you repeat yourself, just keep the pen moving and something new will pop out. You could potentially do all these exercises as a list, but some lend themself more and I've noted instructions in those exercises.

Reviewing

It's important - in this context of learning and growing - that you review what you've written. Ideally read it out loud, there's so much power in voicing our thoughts, even if you're alone. But don't worry if that's just too uncomfortable, the journaling will do the heavy lifting. There are some specific questions for each exercise, but for all, you should review these general reflection questions (repeated with each exercise):

General reflection questions

- What do you notice about what you wrote?
- Did you miss anything obvious? Does something particular stand out?
- How do you feel? Is your energy different after writing?
- Are there any words or phrases calling your attention? If so, make a note of them to use for onward prompts another time.
- Are there any beliefs that need to be checked or updated?

I've left a blank page between each exercise to make any notes or do a little writing.

A final pep-talk

Just before you get going, I'd like to offer a few words of encouragement and give you a few things to remember as you work through the exercises.

1. There's no 'wrong' with these exercises, if you're moving your pen on a piece of paper, you're doing 'it' and it will be useful, one way or another.

2. You really do have your own answers, so trust yourself (even if that's "I need more information/help from someone else on this occasion.")

3. Trust yourself. I'm not an expert and no-one else is on the subject of 'you.' If you disagree with something or think you can do something different to that which I've suggested, then go ahead and trust that instinct.

4. You don't have to have confidence that things will get better, just a tiny shred of hope will do.

This was me. I had no confidence in my life changing, mainly because I didn't know how I wanted it to change, or at least I didn't think I did. I do believe I must have had a scrap of hope though, otherwise I wouldn't have bothered to try.

So don't let not knowing that things will be OK stop you. Just keep moving forward, however slowly and you'll get somewhere, I promise.

5. Know that your efforts (however small) will contribute to change further down the line, even if you feel temporarily unsuccessful. Studies have proved this – it's science.

6. Most of all, be patient with yourself and be kind. Don't worry if things don't change immediately. Despite popular self-help books, some things take time, their own time and whilst some things are simply about making a different choice, some things may be more complex and take a bit more unpicking.

LIFE MANIFESTO

The first set of exercises are under a heading I like to call, *Life Manifesto*. When I work with people, there are some things that come up time and time again. Things that are in the way of people having the life they want.

I'd like to invite you to develop your *Life Manifesto* as a first step before you tackle some of the different aspects, e.g., career, relationships, etc. It may just give you some of the answers you're looking for and it gives you a chance to challenge out of date beliefs along the way.

There are seven exercises in this section to help you explore what you think about life, the Universe and almost everything. For example, what do you expect in life? And whose permission do you need?

Once you've answered these questions, bring the outputs together and make up your *Life Manifesto*. By that I just mean a statement; an intention. Include what you write from each of the exercises as it is, or make it snappier by giving it a little edit, or maybe making a list of bullet point statements, it's up to you.

Begin with, 'I [your name] believe that…'

The exercises in this section are as follows:

1. Hostile or friendly Universe?
2. What do you expect?
3. What do you think?
4. What do you deserve?
5. Whose agenda are you on?
6. Definition of success
7. Permission
8. Thanks (Gratitude)

Life Manifesto

HOSTILE OR FRIENDLY UNIVERSE?

"The most important decision we make is whether we believe we live in a friendly or hostile universe."

Einstein

I flipping love a good, philosophical quote. This is an enormous and powerful question and it's really interesting to explore if you've never thought about it. Take a few minutes to respond, what do you believe?

Prompt: The Universe is …

Free-writing rules

- Set a timer for five minutes so you can let go into the journaling (you can always write more if you want to).
- Keep your pen moving (no editing or looking back) and follow your own emerging topic, even if it's about something else, it will still be important.
- If you get stuck, repeat the prompt or the last two words you wrote, if you feel resistance, annoyance or anything else, write about that.
- If you bump into difficult feelings, either write about them in detail (what does it feel like, where in your body can you feel it, what colour, texture, shape is it, etc.) or make a note to come back to it later when you have the support you need. Refer to the 'It's all about you' section for more.

General reflection questions

- What do you notice about what you wrote?
- Did you miss anything obvious?
- Does something particular stand out?
- How do you feel? Is your energy different after writing?
- Are there any words or phrases calling your attention? If so, make a note of them to use for onward prompts another time.
- Are there any beliefs that need to be checked or updated?

Specific reflection questions

- What does what you wrote tell you about how you see the world?
- Does what you think need some further exploration?

NOTES

Life Manifesto

WHAT DO YOU EXPECT?

"Do you know what happens when you stop settling for less? You get more."

Quote from the film, *Unbelievable*

This is a quote from a film called *Unbelievable*. The context very roughly, was a lawyer talking to a female victim of a crime. She wanted to settle to have it over with and this was his reply to her.

It had a huge impact on me. Such a simple message. Like the other exercises in this section, it's about what you choose in life, and it's a reminder that you can, choose.

What do you expect from life? The bare minimum, everything? Do you expect to succeed, to get by? There's so much within this question, see what comes up for you.

Prompt: In life, I expect …

Free-writing rules

- Set a timer for five minutes so you can let go into the journaling (you can always write more if you want to).
- Keep your pen moving (no editing or looking back) and follow your own emerging topic, even if it's about something else, it will still be important.
- If you get stuck, repeat the prompt or the last two words you wrote, if you feel resistance, annoyance or anything else, write about that.

- If you bump into difficult feelings, either write about them in detail (what does it feel like, where in your body can you feel it, what colour, texture, shape is it, etc.) or make a note to come back to it later when you have the support you need. Refer to the 'It's all about you' section for more.

General reflection questions

- What do you notice about what you wrote?
- Did you miss anything obvious?
- Does something particular stand out?
- How do you feel? Is your energy different after writing?
- Are there any words or phrases calling your attention? If so, make a note of them to use for onward prompts another time.
- Are there any beliefs that need to be checked or updated?

Specific reflection questions

- What does what you wrote tell you about what you expect from life?
- What stories are you telling yourself about your life?

NOTES

Life Manifesto

WHAT DO YOU BELIEVE?

"Life is really simple, but we insist on making it complicated."

Confucius

This exercise is great for stepping back and exploring where you stand on a particular topic. So, for example, you may want to explore your career or romantic love.

For this exercise though, you're going to tackle 'life' as a whole. I know, I like to challenge you.

Take a moment and just see what your beliefs and feelings are about life. Is all life equal? Does each life matter? Is life hard, to be enjoyed?

Prompt: I believe that life is …

Free-writing rules

- Set a timer for five minutes so you can let go into the journaling (you can always write more if you want to).
- Keep your pen moving (no editing or looking back) and follow your own emerging topic, even if it's about something else, it will still be important.
- If you get stuck, repeat the prompt or the last two words you wrote, if you feel resistance, annoyance or anything else, write about that.

- If you bump into difficult feelings, either write about them in detail (what does it feel like, where in your body can you feel it, what colour, texture, shape is it, etc.) or make a note to come back to it later when you have the support you need. Refer to the 'It's all about you' section for more.

General reflection questions

- What do you notice about what you wrote?
- Did you miss anything obvious?
- Does something particular stand out?
- How do you feel? Is your energy different after writing?
- Are there any words or phrases calling your attention? If so, make a note of them to use for onward prompts another time.
- Are there any beliefs that need to be checked or updated?

Specific reflection questions

- Do you think what you believe is true, is a fact, or could it be that there are different opinions and ways to live? If so, are you interested in finding out more?
- Does this affect what you thought you wanted?

NOTES

Life Manifesto

WHAT DO YOU DESERVE?

"There is no vision until you decide what you deserve & staple it to your eyeballs."

Curtis Tyrone Jones

Ooh, another biggie. Again, you can use this when you're focusing on something specific like career, or relationships, but for your *Life Manifesto* you're going to think more broadly. What do you deserve? What does anyone deserve?

Prompt: In life, I deserve...

Free-writing rules

- Set a timer for five minutes so you can let go into the journaling (you can always write more if you want to).
- Keep your pen moving (no editing or looking back) and follow your own emerging topic, even if it's about something else, it will still be important.
- If you get stuck, repeat the prompt or the last two words you wrote, if you feel resistance, annoyance or anything else, write about that.
- If you bump into difficult feelings, either write about them in detail (what does it feel like, where in your body can you feel it, what colour, texture, shape is it, etc.) or make a note to come back to it later when

you have the support you need. Refer to the 'It's all about you' section for more.

General reflection questions

- What do you notice about what you wrote?
- Did you miss anything obvious?
- Does something particular stand out?
- How do you feel? Is your energy different after writing?
- Are there any words or phrases calling your attention? If so, make a note of them to use for onward prompts another time.
- Are there any beliefs that need to be checked or updated?

Specific reflection questions

- Are you deserving of the things you want, and if not, why not? Can this be changed?
- Do other people deserve more/less than you and if so, why?

NOTES

Life Manifesto

WHOSE AGENDA ARE YOU ON?

"Whose agenda are you on Claire?"

My old boss

I was asked this question by an old boss – as it turned out, my answer was that I was entirely on her agenda. At the time, I didn't have my own, but realising that I was at the mercy of someone else's gave me pause.

It wasn't until much later that I developed mine, but I do believe that moment contributed to my prioritising it.

Again, you can apply this to work, home, career etc., but here, think about your overall life.

Prompt: Whose agenda am I on?

Free-writing rules

- Set a timer for five minutes so you can let go into the journaling (you can always write more if you want to).
- Keep your pen moving (no editing or looking back) and follow your own emerging topic, even if it's about something else, it will still be important.
- If you get stuck, repeat the prompt or the last two words you wrote, if you feel resistance, annoyance or anything else, write about that.

- If you bump into difficult feelings, either write about them in detail (what does it feel like, where in your body can you feel it, what colour, texture, shape is it, etc.) or make a note to come back to it later when you have the support you need. Refer to the 'It's all about you' section for more.

General reflection questions

- What do you notice about what you wrote?
- Did you miss anything obvious?
- Does something particular stand out?
- How do you feel? Is your energy different after writing?
- Are there any words or phrases calling your attention? If so, make a note of them to use for onward prompts another time.
- Are there any beliefs that need to be checked or updated?

Specific reflection questions

- How many agendas are you on? Are any of them actually yours?
- Whose expectations are you living up to, or down to?

NOTES

Life Manifesto

DEFINITION OF SUCCESS

"Success is liking yourself, liking what you do, and liking how you do it."

Maya Angelou

We're all influenced by external forces that dictate what success looks like. It's really, really hard not to get wrapped up in it. The pressure to meet these standards can often lead us to what the AA (Alcoholics Anonymous) describe as *Comparing and despairing.*

We compare ourselves all the time. We assume that other people have life all worked out or that it's somehow easier for them. I have two great examples that made me really get that this isn't true.

They have life sorted ...

When I was in London, I shared a house briefly with a CEO who was relocating to a new flat – just for during the week whilst she was in town. She was very impressive, formidable even. I imagined she had life completely sorted - right up until the moment she texted me to ask me if she'd left her straighteners on. "She's just like me!" I thought with relief.

Before I'd felt a bit intimidated by her success; her multiple homes, her CEO role, her family and brimming confidence. But we can't see each other's internal landscapes and the truth is, we're all far more similar than we imagine. The content may be different, but our anxieties, worries, neurosis, I promise, are pretty universal.

It's easier for *Them* because....

I have a friend who exercises every single day, early in the morning. She runs marathons, runs up mountains, she runs a lot. I always assumed she was motivated to do all the training and that it was easy for her. But, during a weekend away, I discovered that she still puts her kit out, on the bed, ready for the next morning so she doesn't have time to negotiate and do something else instead, another reason for her exercising first thing.

I was astounded by this, I genuinely thought - for years by the way - that she just sprang out of bed, excited to get started. But she too has days when she'd really rather stay in bed. Whilst I'm not interested in running up mountains, this really helped me to understand that everyone just has to find their way to get themselves to take action, whatever that may be.

My favourite antidote to comparing and despairing is, *if you're going to compare, compare everything*. Even when you get a peek into someone else's internal landscape, you generally don't know what else is going on in their life.

I didn't know what was going on at home for the CEO I mentioned, what it was that drove her to have that fabulous job? What price was she paying to have the life she had? The full picture may not be so desirable. So until you know everything, think twice about comparing.

Another great antidote is to stop and think about what your definition of success is. Yes, you get to decide! You may need a few tries at this if you've never considered it before, so take your time and come back to it if you need to.

Prompt: Success is ...

Free-writing rules

- Set a timer for five minutes so you can let go into the journaling (you can always write more if you want to).
- Keep your pen moving (no editing or looking back) and follow your own emerging topic, even if it's about something else, it will still be important.
- If you get stuck, repeat the prompt or the last two words you wrote, if you feel resistance, annoyance or anything else, write about that.
- If you bump into difficult feelings, either write about them in detail (what does it feel like, where in your body can you feel it, what colour, texture, shape is it, etc.) or make a note to come back to it later when you have the support you need. Refer to the 'It's all about you' section for more.

You could also do this exercise as a list.

In a list, you repeat the prompt each time followed by your response. It doesn't matter if you repeat yourself, just keep the pen moving and something new will pop out.

General reflection questions

- What do you notice about what you wrote?
- Did you miss anything obvious?
- Does something particular stand out?
- How do you feel? Is your energy different after writing?
- Are there any words or phrases calling your attention? If so, make a note of them to use for onward prompts another time.
- Are there any beliefs that need to be checked or updated?

Specific reflection questions

- Do you feel your definition is really yours?
- As with the question about whose agenda are you on, whose expectations are you measuring your success by?
- Does this affect what you thought you wanted?

NOTES

Life Manifesto

PERMISSION

"Give yourself permission to honour your life."

Elizabeth Gilbert

Whose permission do you need? To do the things you want and live the life you want to live? I attended Liz Gilbert's *Big Magic* workshop (based on her book of the same name) in which she encouraged us to give ourselves permission for our creative endeavours, and I did.

Straight after the workshop, I set up my first journaling workshop – I'd spent a few years thinking about it and doing nothing. I now talk a lot about permission, inspired by this experience, and I find that most people – once they ask the question - don't need anyone's permission but their own. I hope you'll realise it too.

So, stop and think about it now, either in a more general way – about how you live your life – or around something specific. Creativity is often a good example of something people have been told they're not allowed to be.

Prompt: I give myself permission to …

Free-writing rules

- Set a timer for five minutes so you can let go into the journaling (you can always write more if you want to).

- Keep your pen moving (no editing or looking back) and follow your own emerging topic, even if it's about something else, it will still be important.
- If you get stuck, repeat the prompt or the last two words you wrote, if you feel resistance, annoyance or anything else, write about that.
- If you bump into difficult feelings, either write about them in detail (what does it feel like, where in your body can you feel it, what colour, texture, shape is it, etc.) or make a note to come back to it later when you have the support you need. Refer to the 'It's all about you' section for more.

General reflection questions

- What do you notice about what you wrote?
- Did you miss anything obvious?
- Does something particular stand out?
- How do you feel? Is your energy different after writing?
- Are there any words or phrases calling your attention? If so, make a note of them to use for onward prompts another time.
- Are there any beliefs that need to be checked or updated?

Specific reflection questions

- Whose permission do you need?
- Can you give yourself permission and if not, what do you need to get it?

Life Manifesto

THANK YOU (GRATITUDE)

"Let us be grateful to the people who make us happy; they are the charming gardeners who make our souls blossom."

Marcel Proust

One thing consistent across self-help, psychology, philosophy and religious teachings, is the idea that if you can be grateful for what you have, you will not only be happier, but be more receptive to changing whatever it is that's not working for you, which is why I've included a bit of gratitude here in the manifesto.

I invite you to pick someone who makes your life better and write them an imaginary thank you letter telling them everything you love about them. You don't have to choose a romantic relationship for this exercise or even someone you know. You may also prefer to write to your cat, to Mother Nature or to your favourite pyjamas. Tell them how and why you love them: How do they make you feel? What is it that they do that other people don't? What do they know about you or see in you?

Prompt: Dear [name], thank you …

Free-writing rules

- Set a timer for five minutes so you can let go into the journaling (you can always write more if you want to).
- Keep your pen moving (no editing or looking back) and follow your own emerging topic, even if it's about something else, it will still be important.

- If you get stuck, repeat the prompt or the last two words you wrote, if you feel resistance, annoyance or anything else, write about that.
- If you bump into difficult feelings, either write about them in detail (what does it feel like, where in your body can you feel it, what colour, texture, shape is it, etc.) or make a note to come back to it later when you have the support you need. Refer to the 'It's all about you' section for more.

General reflection questions

- What do you notice about what you wrote?
- Did you miss anything obvious?
- Does something particular stand out?
- How do you feel? Is your energy different after writing?
- Are there any words or phrases calling your attention? If so, make a note of them to use for onward prompts another time.
- Are there any beliefs that need to be checked or updated?

Specific reflection questions

- Do you think the object of your thanks knows how you feel?
- Is there anyone else you'd like to thank? This is a really nice thing to incorporate into your regular journaling, maybe once a week and remember, you can write to anything or anyone.

You now have all the content you need to make your Life Manifesto. You can keep it as it is, edit it down to a short paragraph or write it as a list; I will, I believe, etc.

I recommend starting by writing:

This is my Life Manifesto and I [name], state the following:

The universe is…

I expect…

I think that life…

I deserve…

I'm on [whose?] agenda…

My definition of success is…

I give myself permission to…

NOTES

WARMING UP

You're now into the main exercises.

I generally use a warm-up in workshops to bring people into the moment, so in case you just want to start off with something simpler to ease you in, here are a few warm-up exercises.

You can also use these for general journaling.

Warming up

BRAIN DUMP

This is a great exercise and is essentially just straight journaling.

Just splurging onto the page can often help you to make sense of what's happening, and even come up with solutions without searching for them. 'Getting it all out' is also a great way to self-soothe and release the energy that goes with over-thinking and overload.

Prompt: What's currently happening is ...

Free-writing rules

- Set a timer for five minutes so you can let go into the journaling (you can always write more if you want to).
- Keep your pen moving (no editing or looking back) and follow your own emerging topic, even if it's about something else, it will still be important.
- If you get stuck, repeat the prompt or the last two words you wrote, if you feel resistance, annoyance or anything else, write about that.
- If you bump into difficult feelings, either write about them in detail (what does it feel like, where in your body can you feel it, what colour, texture, shape is it, etc.) or make a note to come back to it later when you have the support you need. Refer to the 'It's all about you' section for more.

General reflection questions

- What do you notice about what you wrote?
- Did you miss anything obvious?
- Does something particular stand out?

- How do you feel? Is your energy different after writing?
- Are there any words or phrases calling your attention? If so, make a note of them to use for onward prompts another time.
- Are there any beliefs that need to be checked or updated?

Specific reflection questions

- Was it easy or hard to get started? Do you know why?
- Is there anything that needs attention before you can do some more targeted journaling?

NOTES

Warming Up

SIX SENSES

This grounding exercise will help you to be mindful, to come back to yourself through your senses and 'arrive' in the moment.

How do you feel? What do you see, hear, taste, smell? How does your body feel? Tense, relaxed, soft?

This is also a great exercise for when you're 'in' anxiety, overwhelm or excessive worry and I have a great example.

I was about to deliver a new workshop to a new group of people, in person, right after lockdown. I was prepared and largely calm, but right before the workshop I got into a bit of anxiety. So, I wrote, "I'm anxious," in fast and furious, messy handwriting, letting the energy spill out onto the page. It was big and scrawly and frantic. I described where it was in my body, what it felt like, I really went for it.

Then, I stopped and started writing, slowly and in big solid letters, 'calm' and 'slow' and 'breathe.' I kept repeating these words with a bit more description, making myself go slowly and calmly.

It worked extremely well. I'd never done this before, it just sort of happened. I calmed right down and, of course, the workshop went really well. I guess some of it is just about getting the energy out and, in this case, onto the page.

Prompt: I feel... I see... I hear... I smell... I taste... I sense...

List: In a list, you repeat the prompt each time followed by your response. It doesn't matter if you repeat yourself, just keep the pen moving and something new will pop out.

Free-writing rules

- Set a timer for five minutes so you can let go into the journaling (you can always write more if you want to).
- Keep your pen moving (no editing or looking back) and follow your own emerging topic, even if it's about something else, it will still be important.
- If you get stuck, repeat the prompt or the last two words you wrote, if you feel resistance, annoyance or anything else, write about that.
- If you bump into difficult feelings, either write about them in detail (what does it feel like, where in your body can you feel it, what colour, texture, shape is it, etc.) or make a note to come back to it later when you have the support you need. Refer to the 'It's all about you' section for more.

General reflection questions

- What do you notice about what you wrote?
- Did you miss anything obvious?
- Does something particular stand out?
- How do you feel? Is your energy different after writing?
- Are there any words or phrases calling your attention? If so, make a note of them to use for onward prompts another time.
- Are there any beliefs that need to be checked or updated?

Prompt specific reflections:

- Where is your attention most focused?
- Are you surprised by how much/little you're feeling?

NOTES

Warming Up

BIBLE DIP (it doesn't have to be a bible)

This is great for warming up or general journaling. *Bible dip* comes from Augusten Burroughs brilliant book, *Running with Scissors*. One of Augusten's pseudo-adopted sisters takes to sticking her finger in the bible and letting the phrase she lands on answer a question or make a decision for her.

Here you're just going to use what you land on as a starting point. You can choose any material; a book, a magazine, a menu, anything with words on it. Close your eyes and stick your finger on some text on a random page. Then you use that text (a word or a sentence) as your starting prompt.

Prompt: Word or sentence you land on ...

Free-writing rules

- Set a timer for five minutes so you can let go into the journaling (you can always write more if you want to).
- Keep your pen moving (no editing or looking back) and follow your own emerging topic, even if it's about something else, it will still be important.
- If you get stuck, repeat the prompt or the last two words you wrote, if you feel resistance, annoyance or anything else, write about that.
- If you bump into difficult feelings, either write about them in detail (what does it feel like, where in your body can you feel it, what colour, texture, shape is it, etc.) or make a note to come back to it later when you have the support you need. Refer to the 'It's all about you' section for more.

General reflection questions

- What do you notice about what you wrote?
- Did you miss anything obvious?
- Does something particular stand out?
- How do you feel? Is your energy different after writing?
- Are there any words or phrases calling your attention? If so, make a note of them to use for onward prompts another time.
- Are there any beliefs that need to be checked or updated?

Specific reflection questions

- Did you wish you'd picked something else?
- Was there something you picked first and then moved on from that you're now curious about? What was it? Could you write from it now?

NOTES

WHAT'S HAPPENING NOW?

A lot of coaching models would have you start with the goal. I prefer that you have that goal in mind, but start with what's happening now, in your particular situation. What's making you want the thing you're aiming for. What's missing, what's happening/not happening? Who is involved? There are lots of questions and some of the answers may or may not make you rethink your goal.

As I mentioned before, it's my experience, and that of many coaches, that what people say they want in the beginning often tends to be what they 'think' they want, or should want, and further exploration reveals a different, if connected need.

It's not to say you're wrong, it's just that we often make assumptions about what 'x' will give us and we all need to probe a little bit in order to find out if that's really true.

What's happening now?

INTO THE WEEDS

Here you're going to write, in as much detail as possible, what's happening in your particular situation. For example, you may be unhappy with your job, feel you're in a rut, or struggling in a relationship.

Get granular. If you're a 'who dunnit' fan, get your Sherlock hat on and your magnifying glass out. Who is involved? When does it happen? What's happening just before/just after? Take as long as you need to get it all down.

This exercise is also great for externalising the spin-cycle and grounding yourself into the present.

Prompt: What's happening is …

Free-writing rules

- Set a timer for five minutes so you can let go into the journaling (you can always write more if you want to).
- Keep your pen moving (no editing or looking back) and follow your own emerging topic, even if it's about something else, it will still be important.
- If you get stuck, repeat the prompt or the last two words you wrote, if you feel resistance, annoyance or anything else, write about that.
- If you bump into difficult feelings, either write about them in detail (what does it feel like, where in your body can you feel it, what colour, texture, shape is it, etc.) or make a note to come back to it later when you have the support you need. Refer to the 'It's all about you' section for more.

General reflection questions

- What do you notice about what you wrote?
- Did you miss anything obvious?
- Does something particular stand out?
- How do you feel? Is your energy different after writing?
- Are there any words or phrases calling your attention? If so, make a note of them to use for onward prompts another time.
- Are there any beliefs that need to be checked or updated?

Specific reflection questions

- Is the problem what you thought? Could it be something else and if so, do you know what?
- How much are you assuming?
- Are you generalising about anything? We all do this so don't feel bad, what's important is to notice it as that's where useful information lies.

NOTES

What's happening now?

FROM THE MOUNTAIN TOP

This is similar to *Into the Weeds* (can be interesting to do both) except you're going to imagine sitting on a mountain top and looking down at your life unfolding below. What you see is your life in miniature unfolding.

Prompt: From up here ...

Free-writing rules

- Set a timer for five minutes so you can let go into the journaling (you can always write more if you want to).
- Keep your pen moving (no editing or looking back) and follow your own emerging topic, even if it's about something else, it will still be important.
- If you get stuck, repeat the prompt or the last two words you wrote, if you feel resistance, annoyance or anything else, write about that.
- If you bump into difficult feelings, either write about them in detail (what does it feel like, where in your body can you feel it, what colour, texture, shape is it, etc.) or make a note to come back to it later when you have the support you need. Refer to the 'It's all about you' section for more.

General reflection questions

- What do you notice about what you wrote?
- Did you miss anything obvious?
- Does something particular stand out?
- How do you feel? Is your energy different after writing?
- Are there any words or phrases calling your attention? If so, make a note of them to use for onward prompts another time.

- Are there any beliefs that need to be checked or updated?

Specific reflection questions

- How did you feel, looking down on your life?
- If you also did 'Into the Weeds' what was different looking from above?

NOTES

What's happening now?

NEWSPAPER ARTICLE

Imagine that someone is reporting on your situation in the newspaper. However ridiculous that may seem, try and take a leap. What would you see written down? Don't overthink it, just pick up your pen and give it a go.

I like to be a bit over-dramatic in this exercise. It helps me to not take myself too seriously but it also helps me to see things in a different light. So, whatever your natural tendency, see if you can do the opposite.

Pick a headline for your article, for example: 'Woman struggles over difficult decision about which outfit fits 'smart/casual' for upcoming conference (This actually did happen to me recently – my solution? Take everything.)

This exercise came from the very first free-writing workshop I attended called, 'Free fall: Writing as creative therapy.' I've pulled out one section of a longer exercise on dealing with difficult memories.

Prompt: Article headline …

Free-writing rules

- Set a timer for five minutes so you can let go into the journaling (you can always write more if you want to).
- Keep your pen moving (no editing or looking back) and follow your own emerging topic, even if it's about something else, it will still be important.
- If you get stuck, repeat the prompt or the last two words you wrote, if you feel resistance, annoyance or anything else, write about that.

- If you bump into difficult feelings, either write about them in detail (what does it feel like, where in your body can you feel it, what colour, texture, shape is it, etc.) or make a note to come back to it later when you have the support you need. Refer to the 'It's all about you' section for more.

General reflection questions

- What do you notice about what you wrote?
- Did you miss anything obvious?
- Does something particular stand out?
- How do you feel? Is your energy different after writing?
- Are there any words or phrases calling your attention? If so, make a note of them to use for onward prompts another time.
- Are there any beliefs that need to be checked or updated?

Specific reflection questions

- Were you able to be dramatic and take a big step back?
- Is there another headline that gives a different spin that you could write this exercise from?

NOTES

GOALS – EXPLORING

Now that you've done a bit of digging into what's actually going on, you may now be clearer on what it is you want, or don't want.

If that's you, jump straight to the next section, *Goals – Clarifying*.

Exploring what you want

If you don't know, don't worry. It's very common to be stuck not wanting what you have but not knowing what to do next.

Also, not knowing what you want can be the very thing that stops you doing anything at all. The result is that you stay stuck and frustrated. I've been a victim of this and as I say, it's something that's very easy to fall into.

Taking action, exploring, trying something out and getting feedback is key to moving forward. I was told this – and ignored it – for years. But eventually the penny dropped, so if I can convince you of anything, it's this.

Spend some time here, exploring what you might want. It's also worth going back to the *Life Manifesto* section if you've not done it already as this can surface surprising answers.

Don't expect big shiny answers, if there were some, you'd have them by now. You'll likely start with small clues that you'll need to follow, like pulling on a thread, to see if there's something there.

Here are a few exercises for you to do just this.

Exploring what you want

IF I LIVED FOREVER

You've probably come across the exercise, or answered the question, "What if you only had 'x' amount of time to live?" I find this is a bit restrictive.

I prefer to ask, "What if you lived forever?" Taking away the restriction of time opens up so many more possibilities.

It no longer matters how long something may take, learning the piano for example, or how many things you might want to do.

You could technically say, "Everything." Learn every profession, every instrument, every skill etc. That may be true for you and if it is, is this restricting you? You don't start at all because there's simply not enough time?

Prompt: If I lived forever …

Free-writing rules

- Set a timer for five minutes so you can let go into the journaling (you can always write more if you want to).
- Keep your pen moving (no editing or looking back) and follow your own emerging topic, even if it's about something else, it will still be important.
- If you get stuck, repeat the prompt or the last two words you wrote, if you feel resistance, annoyance or anything else, write about that.
- If you bump into difficult feelings, either write about them in detail (what does it feel like, where in your body can you feel it, what colour, texture, shape is it, etc.) or make a note to come back to it later when you have the support you need. Refer to the 'It's all about you' section for more.

General reflection questions

- What do you notice about what you wrote?
- Did you miss anything obvious?
- Does something particular stand out?
- How do you feel? Is your energy different after writing?
- Are there any words or phrases calling your attention? If so, make a note of them to use for onward prompts another time.
- Are there any beliefs that need to be checked or updated?

Specific reflection questions

- What sort of things came up, is there a theme?
- Did this exercise make you anxious or excited?
- You'll likely notice a theme or two running through what you've written, what clues can you take from this?
- Is there one thing that you could try, even if it doesn't seem like the exact answer?

NOTES

Exploring what you want

ALTERNATIVE LIVES

I love this exercise which comes from Julia Cameron's widely read book, *The Artist's Way.*

I've done this exercise several times and it's really enlightening. It's fun to do just for the sake of it, but really helpful if you're not sure what you want next for yourself and your life or even unsure about who you are.

First, list several *Alternative lives* that appeal to you, ideally two or three. Don't let reality get in the way. It may be something you saw in a film, it may be a lifestyle or profession that doesn't exist anymore, or never did, if you can imagine it, it's in.

Now pick one (if you're working with someone else, have them pick one for you) and write as if this is now your life. Totally 'go there.'

You're not wondering if you can here, or thinking about why you can't, you just transport yourself to this other life and are now living it. What's it like? What are you doing? Who are you with? How do you feel? Really let go into it.

Prompt: I'm a ...

Free-writing rules

- Set a timer for five minutes so you can let go into the journaling (you can always write more if you want to).
- Keep your pen moving (no editing or looking back) and follow your own emerging topic, even if it's about something else, it will still be important.

- If you get stuck, repeat the prompt or the last two words you wrote, if you feel resistance, annoyance or anything else, write about that.
- If you bump into difficult feelings, either write about them in detail (what does it feel like, where in your body can you feel it, what colour, texture, shape is it, etc.) or make a note to come back to it later when you have the support you need. Refer to the 'It's all about you' section for more.

General reflection questions

- What do you notice about what you wrote?
- Did you miss anything obvious?
- Does something particular stand out?
- How do you feel? Is your energy different after writing?
- Are there any words or phrases calling your attention? If so, make a note of them to use for onward prompts another time.
- Are there any beliefs that need to be checked or updated?

Specific reflection questions

- What does this life tell you about what you might want more or less of? If you do this more than once you'll start to see themes.
- Do you want to do this with the other lives you wrote down, if so, go for it!

NOTES

Exploring what you want

'WOULDN'T IT BE LOVELY?'

I like to think of the song from *My Fair Lady* when I'm doing this exercise. Eliza Doolittle sings about all the things that would be lovely; if she lived in a nice warm house with nice things. She really indulges in the detail of what she wants.

Of course, you don't have to rhyme, but if that's what happens, then so be it. I rapped my free-writing for a short period and never really worked out what that was about, but it was fun.

Also, you don't need to know what 'it' is, you can just focus on how you want to feel and experience either in a particular area, or in your life generally. I sometimes do this exercise out loud (quietly of course) as I'm on my daily walk. I recommend doing this exercise as a list, but of course, you can do a straight free-write.

List: In a list, you repeat the prompt each time followed by your response. It doesn't matter if you repeat yourself, just keep the pen moving and something new will pop out

Prompt: Wouldn't it be lovely …

Free-writing rules

- Set a timer for five minutes so you can let go into the journaling (you can always write more if you want to).
- Keep your pen moving (no editing or looking back) and follow your own emerging topic, even if it's about something else, it will still be important.
- If you get stuck, repeat the prompt or the last two words you wrote, if you feel resistance, annoyance or anything else, write about that.

- If you bump into difficult feelings, either write about them in detail (what does it feel like, where in your body can you feel it, what colour, texture, shape is it, etc.) or make a note to come back to it later when you have the support you need. Refer to the 'It's all about you' section for more.

General reflection questions

- What do you notice about what you wrote?
- Did you miss anything obvious?
- Does something particular stand out?
- How do you feel? Is your energy different after writing?
- Are there any words or phrases calling your attention? If so, make a note of them to use for onward prompts another time.
- Are there any beliefs that need to be checked or updated?

Specific reflection questions

- Were you able to just play with the idea of what would be lovely?
- Did reality creep in? If so, you can keep trying again until you get past that natural tendency.

NOTES

GOALS – CLARIFYING

Once you know what you want, it's time to do a bit of interrogating to check that it's the right thing and that you're clear. This can change as the process moves forward and you dig a little deeper each time. That's OK, as long as you're not sabotaging yourself and jumping from one thing to another, evolution is often part of the process.

It's tempting to think, "But I know what I want, I don't need to do this." This may be true, but experience (with myself and others) has shown me that this part is vital and can reveal small but significant aspects of what you're aiming for, if not, alter it completely. The more resistance you feel the more likely it is that there is something to uncover.

So, take a few minutes to do at least one of these exercises. You won't regret it.

Goals - Clarifying

EXPLAIN YOURSELF

For this exercise, I'd like you to choose a grandparent and/or a child. They could be related to you, real or fictional, dead or alive, it's up to you.

This is about getting clarity on your chosen goal (or solution) and to do this, you're going to explain it to your chosen grandparent and/or child. I'd recommend doing both as they will bring out different perspectives.

Writing to different audiences can change not just the tone of what you write, but the words you write too. Explaining more complex things to someone who sees the world in a simpler way is a sure-fire way to find out if you're clear about what it is you want to do. You can discover holes in your plan, areas that are less clear and more. Write to them and tell them, nice and simply what it is you're going to do and why.

If you feel compelled to have your chosen person write back, then go for it. Getting into this kind of back and forth (dialoguing) and harnessing the different perspectives you have within you is probably the most useful thing you can do. They may have questions or just comments about what you've just written.

Another extension of this exercise is to ask an expert. Someone who knows all about the topic you're talking about.

This exercise can actually be used at any stage in the process as a way to check in with yourself.

Prompt: I'd like to tell you about ...

Free-writing rules

- Set a timer for five minutes so you can let go into the journaling (you can always write more if you want to).
- Keep your pen moving (no editing or looking back) and follow your own emerging topic, even if it's about something else, it will still be important.
- If you get stuck, repeat the prompt or the last two words you wrote, if you feel resistance, annoyance or anything else, write about that.
- If you bump into difficult feelings, either write about them in detail (what does it feel like, where in your body can you feel it, what colour, texture, shape is it, etc.) or make a note to come back to it later when you have the support you need. Refer to the 'It's all about you' section for more.

General reflection questions

- What do you notice about what you wrote?
- Did you miss anything obvious?
- Does something particular stand out?
- How do you feel? Is your energy different after writing?
- Are there any words or phrases calling your attention? If so, make a note of them to use for onward prompts another time.
- Are there any beliefs that need to be checked or updated?

Specific reflection questions

- Were you able to explain yourself?
- Are *you* clear? Keep trying until you can explain it more simply.

NOTES

Goals – Clarifying

MANIFEST MEMOIR

I'm asking you to take another leap with me here. Whether you believe in universal manifesting or not, this exercise will stretch your imagination to what's possible and open your energy to what you want (this is how I think about manifesting).

You're going to write about what's happening now that your difficult relationship has got better, you've been promoted, escaped from your crippling career, got married, are working three days a week, or whatever your goal is.

Really 'go there' and imagine what it feels like, what's happening around you, what's not happening, what are you're doing, how are people interacting with you etc. This is great even if you don't know what you want exactly but you know how you want to feel.

So, for example, you may want more love in your life. You may be open to how that comes to you – it doesn't always have to be romantic after all. You can just talk about how it feels to be loved and how you know that you are. Go really 'large' here, don't hold back. The bigger you can expand our imagination the more possibilities you'll open up.

Prompt: It's really happening …

Free-writing rules

- Set a timer for five minutes so you can let go into the journaling (you can always write more if you want to).
- Keep your pen moving (no editing or looking back) and follow your own emerging topic, even if it's about something else, it will still be important.

- If you get stuck, repeat the prompt or the last two words you wrote, if you feel resistance, annoyance or anything else, write about that.
- If you bump into difficult feelings, either write about them in detail (what does it feel like, where in your body can you feel it, what colour, texture, shape is it, etc.) or make a note to come back to it later when you have the support you need. Refer to the 'It's all about you' section for more.

General reflection questions

- What do you notice about what you wrote?
- Did you miss anything obvious?
- Does something particular stand out?
- How do you feel? Is your energy different after writing?
- Are there any words or phrases calling your attention? If so, make a note of them to use for onward prompts another time.
- Are there any beliefs that need to be checked or updated?

Specific reflection questions

- How did it make you feel to make a leap? Or if you were unable to, can you say why?
- Do you believe you can have the things you want, the life you want? If you've not done it already, perhaps take a look at the 'Life Manifesto' section.
- If you surface major blocks here, like, "I don't deserve it," or "it doesn't happen to 'people like me,' explore those things and see how you feel about the possibility of that changing. If you don't unpick and reframe them, they'll likely get in the way somewhere down the line.
- Is the goal the right one, or might it be something slightly different, i.e. 'I want to spend more time writing just for enjoyment' might become, 'I want to have more fun, full stop' which may lead into 'I want a better work/life balance.'

NOTES

Goals - Clarifying

30 WORDS

This is a great little exercise, often used in creative writing. It's useful for lots of things where a 'sum-up' is required. It's really great for clarifying your goal – succinctly.

You're going to just look back over what you've written up until this point and pull out six or seven words that particularly resonate with you.

Don't overthink it, just pick them instinctively. Now, just write a few lines and include the words and phrases you've picked out in any order. It can be less than 30 words but no more. Do this quite quickly without thinking too much. You can edit it later but just doing that quick summary can be extremely helpful.

Start with one of the words or phrases you've picked out.

Prompt: Word/phrase you chose ...

Free-writing rules

- Set a timer for five minutes so you can let go into the journaling (you can always write more if you want to).
- Keep your pen moving (no editing or looking back) and follow your own emerging topic, even if it's about something else, it will still be important.
- If you get stuck, repeat the prompt or the last two words you wrote, if you feel resistance, annoyance or anything else, write about that.
- If you bump into difficult feelings, either write about them in detail (what does it feel like, where in your body can you feel it, what colour, texture, shape is it, etc.) or make a note

to come back to it later when you have the support you need. Refer to the 'It's all about you' section for more.

General reflection questions

- What do you notice about what you wrote?
- Did you miss anything obvious?
- Does something particular stand out?
- How do you feel? Is your energy different after writing?
- Are there any words or phrases calling your attention? If so, make a note of them to use for onward prompts another time.
- Are there any beliefs that need to be checked or updated?

Specific reflection questions

- How does your summary make you feel?
- Is there anything missing?

NOTES

OPTIONS

Once you know what you want, it's time to look at options – all the things you could do – and pick one.

So first, list as many options as you can. Don't worry whether or not they seem realistic, desirable, doable. The purpose at this point is just to list as many options as you can. Partly to open up your mind to different possibilities and also to remind yourself that – even when it feels like you don't - you always have a choice. For me, writing this book was part of a bigger goal to share these tools, one option was to write a book, and here we are.

If, for the purposes of a further example, I wanted to lose weight, I can choose from the following options: go on a diet, go to the gym, learn about what food my body needs, join a weight loss group, have coaching, walk every day, etc. There are of course many more options.

NOTE OF CAUTION: It's easy to look at the most obvious option and do that, but take a moment to stop and think, has this worked for you before? What obstacles did you face in choosing this course of action? So, to lose weight, whilst going on a diet seems like the most obvious, if this didn't work for you in the past, is there may be a better way to tackle the problem? For example, first learning about what food is healthy and why?

Once you have your list, choose the option that feels right for you, right now.

This is the easy way; write a load of options and pick one, and sometimes it's that straightforward. Sometimes though, things are a little more complex or it may be more difficult to see your way out/through something.

The next few exercises will help you explore, a bit more broadly what your options may be.

Options

THE LAST THING I'D DO (to actually achieve my goal)

Sometimes it's a lot easier to think of what you wouldn't do in order to achieve something. For example, just watching a load of Netflix is a sure way to 'not' do almost anything, unless of course, watching Netflix is your goal. No judgement.

Some struggle with being negative and can find this exercise a challenge, but if you can push through that and hold it lightly, this can be a great way to come up with options on how to proceed, and often more than if you just wrote possible things you could do. You can then of course flip them into positive steps forward.

Prompt: To make sure [goal] doesn't happen, I'll...

Free-writing rules

- Set a timer for five minutes so you can let go into the journaling (you can always write more if you want to).
- Keep your pen moving (no editing or looking back) and follow your own emerging topic, even if it's about something else, it will still be important.
- If you get stuck, repeat the prompt or the last two words you wrote, if you feel resistance, annoyance or anything else, write about that.
- If you bump into difficult feelings, either write about them in detail (what does it feel like, where in your body can you feel it, what colour, texture, shape is it, etc.) or make a note to come back to it later when you have the support you need. Refer to the 'It's all about you' section for more.

General reflection questions

- What do you notice about what you wrote?
- Did you miss anything obvious?
- Does something particular stand out?
- How do you feel? Is your energy different after writing?
- Are there any words or phrases calling your attention? If so, make a note of them to use for onward prompts another time.
- Are there any beliefs that need to be checked or updated?

Specific reflection questions

- Did you find it hard to be negative? If so, what does this mean to you? How could it be holding you back? For example, if you're not prepared to look at the possible things that get in your way, is it possible that you're not being realistic in your goal setting?
- Were there any ideas you could use if you flip the negatives into positives – things you could do?

NOTES

Options

THE LAST TIME I...

Thinking back to when you might have made a change, achieved something or solved a problem is really valuable. The goal may be different but the way you get there can hold valuable clues to what works for you.

For example, in trying to achieve a significant project at work, someone I coached thought back to when he'd trained for a marathon to remember what had worked for him in terms of planning, training and ultimately, achieving the goal.

What you refer back to could be something really small like finishing a report or project, or changing a small habit. It all holds clues that will help you now.

Prompt: The last time I ...

Free-writing rules

- Set a timer for five minutes so you can let go into the journaling (you can always write more if you want to).
- Keep your pen moving (no editing or looking back) and follow your own emerging topic, even if it's about something else, it will still be important.
- If you get stuck, repeat the prompt or the last two words you wrote, if you feel resistance, annoyance or anything else, write about that.
- If you bump into difficult feelings, either write about them in detail (what does it feel like, where in your body can you feel it, what colour, texture, shape is it, etc.) or make a note to come back to it later when you have the support you need. Refer to the 'It's all about you' section for more.

General reflection questions

- What do you notice about what you wrote?
- Did you miss anything obvious?
- Does something particular stand out?
- How do you feel? Is your energy different after writing?
- Are there any words or phrases calling your attention? If so, make a note of them to use for onward prompts another time.
- Are there any beliefs that need to be checked or updated?

Specific reflection questions

- What components can you pull out from your previous experience, can those same activities help this time?
- Did it make you think of any other examples? Repeat this exercise if so.

NOTES

Options

WHAT DOES THE RADIATOR THINK?

Without doubt, this is the most useful dialoguing exercise.

You're going to get a different perspective via an object; through the imagined voice of that object.

This can feel a little odd, but trust me, you have other voices inside your head – apart from the critic – and this is a great way to surface them. They get to hitch a ride through the object you choose. For example, people often write from a plant, the tone of which tends to be nurturing and caring. Each object will have its own personality and message or advice. Objects will help you to surface inner wisdom, advice, creativity and lots more.

So first, pick an inanimate object from your immediate vicinity that catches your eye.

People have used things ranging from; their pen, their glasses, a stain on the carpet, a plant, an award, a fire extinguisher, a travel pass, flowers, and of course the radiator. There is no limit to what you choose, just trust your instincts and pick what catches your eye.

Now, you're going to have your object comment on the list of options you've come up with so far. Just see what it has to say and if it has anything to add.

Prompt: I'm your [insert object] and I think ...

Free-writing rules

- Set a timer for five minutes so you can let go into the journaling (you can always write more if you want to).

- Keep your pen moving (no editing or looking back) and follow your own emerging topic, even if it's about something else, it will still be important.
- If you get stuck, repeat the prompt or the last two words you wrote, if you feel resistance, annoyance or anything else, write about that.
- If you bump into difficult feelings, either write about them in detail (what does it feel like, where in your body can you feel it, what colour, texture, shape is it, etc.) or make a note to come back to it later when you have the support you need. Refer to the 'It's all about you' section for more.

General reflection questions

- What do you notice about what you wrote?
- Did you miss anything obvious?
- Does something particular stand out?
- How do you feel? Is your energy different after writing?
- Are there any words or phrases calling your attention? If so, make a note of them to use for onward prompts another time.
- Are there any beliefs that need to be checked or updated?

Specific reflection questions

- Are you surprised by what this voice has to say? Is it familiar?
- Do you feel inclined to ask another object?

You can bring in any other voices you've used in previous exercises, e.g., the Nan and Child. You can also ask people you'd love to hear from. What might Oprah say? Or your favourite teacher from junior school? Dead or alive, known or not, they'll channel the part of you that you project onto them.

One of your 'voices' may suggest that you actually need to speak to an actual 'someone' at this stage and that's OK. Surfacing that you need outside help is really useful and it might be easier to hear it from another part of you.

This exercise is great to use when reflecting on anything – so after any of the exercises in this book you could do this one.

You could even have another object comment on what the first object thinks or write back to the object, this exercise has no limits.

NOTES

WHAT'S NEXT?

You're going great guns. You're clear on your goal and you know the course of action you want to take. Now is the time to ask yourself, *What's next?* What is your next action.

We're brilliant at spending oodles of time thinking about what we want, different ways of achieving it, making plans, reading books about how to make those plans happen, etc. But unless we actually ***do*** something, it's unlikely anything will change.

Your *What's next?* should be something really small like booking time in your diary to do some research, or speak to someone for example. Something it's almost impossible to find a reason not to do. A good rule of thumb to make sure you get clear on your *What's next?* is to deploy these five questions in order to get specific:

What are you going to do?

When will you do it? Date and time please, not 'next week.'

Where will you do it? Do you need to book space to do that research or get out in nature to take time to get some headspace before you begin?

Who do you need to help you/do it with? - if appropriate.

How are you going to do it? What might you need to get going in terms of resources: people, information, time etc?

I promise this is worthwhile and totally do-able on your own.

How confident are you?

Now ask yourself how confident you are that you will do it? If you waver and say "I'll try,' are you really committed?" Some coaches won't allow you to use the word 'try' because it's almost inevitably self-defeating. If you can't say "I'll do x, y, z," why not?

If there's doubt, who or what might be getting in the way? How might you mitigate that?

What might make you more likely to do it?

You should be in the 9 or 10 out of 10 area. Again, the action should be so small and do-able that you cannot fail.

If you can drill down to a tiny next step, I promise the giant leaps will follow.

Never leave yourself without a What's next?

When you've taken action, make sure you choose the next *What's next?*

Even if I don't know what my *What's next?* is, working out what my *What's next?* will be the next *What's next?*

In case it's not clear, always have a *What's next?*

NOTES

PLANNING AND MITIGATING

Planning

If you're anything like me and your goal has multiple aspects, you may want to spend a bit of time identifying the various steps and planning what you're going to do and when.

This is great if your goal is more complex, but don't let the planning get in the way of the 'doing' which is another great way to distract yourself. It's something I'm regularly guilty of (the more I catch myself and adjust the less it happens). "Oh, if I can just combine that action list, with that content strategy, everything will be easier." If I had a penny …

Be Agile in your approach. 'Agile' is a project management method where you have your key milestones, but you only get into the details on a weekly basis so that you can adapt your plan along the way.

Mitigating

I spent many years managing projects and programmes and one of the most important steps was to mitigate potential problems. You can't always know what's going to pop up, but there will certainly be things you will know in advance. For me, getting distracted by new and shiny things is always a potential blocker to getting something done, especially if I'm overwhelmed by the enormity of something. This book was guaranteed to trigger this pattern so I needed to think about how I was going to manage it, and that means getting specific, not just saying, "Oh, I'll deal with it."

My blocks for writing this book – and they're probably the same ones for almost everything for me, are:

- Getting distracted by shiny new things ("Ooh, what about a book on journaling for stress and anxiety would be brilliant!" Maybe, but not before I finish this one).
- Jumping ahead to the fun stuff, e.g., design and images.
- Focusing on the things that I don't know about rather than writing the first draft, e.g., the whole publishing process - whether to self-publish or find a publisher.
- Getting overwhelmed by the enormity of the project, "Where to start!? There's too much to do, I can't face it!"

In order to mitigate these potential blockers, I planned the following:

Potential blockers	Mitigation
Getting distracted by shiny new things.	Have a 'car park' for new ideas and put anything that comes up there. This is just a piece of paper called 'car park' with post it notes all over it.
Jumping ahead to the fun stuff; design images etc.	Focus on draft one first. I'm not allowed to look at anything else until I've done this. My Mantra: "Just write the first draft, just write the first draft."
Focusing on the things that I don't know about.	As above – this is guaranteed to get in my way and may even stop me writing the first draft. So back to "Just write the first draft."
Getting overwhelmed by the enormity of the project.	Commit to a really small action. One block of 30 minutes per week. It sounds miniscule but it needs to be manageable. Of course, I can do more, but this way, I'll make slow and steady progress. This is uncomfortable for me, but rushing into

	something saying, "I'll finish it next week!" will guarantee it never gets written. This is what I normally do. One block of 30 minutes, then another. Small, simple. Something I feel totally able to do, whatever kind of week I'm having. Also, if I don't do it, it's only 30 minutes, not an overwhelming thing I'd failed to do, which again, would likely have stopped me taking any action. For each block, just keep my head in the detail, e.g., I'll work on that paragraph or I'll review the exercises for consistency etc.

If you aren't familiar with your blocks, I promise that regular journaling is a great way to start to notice them.

NOTES

TAKING ACTION

As I've mentioned, action is where, well … the action is. All of this work is nothing without it. But this is where most of us (me included) can trip up. There are lots of reasons you might not be taking action.

You may just need a hand to hold to take the first step, or it might be that you're just not quite ready.

Ready or not?

There's a subtle difference between the two and it's not always easy to spot which one is holding you back.

Sometimes you need to get used to the idea of something before you take action or you may need some inspiration.

This was the case for me with my very first journaling group when I still lived in London. There I sat, in a *Pret a Manger* with my little home-made Meetup sign on the table waiting anxiously for someone to come along. I needed a little courage at that stage otherwise I'd never have done it. I'd spent, probably a couple of years working up to that point, thinking about wanting to do it, being afraid etc.

It was finally attending Liz Gilbert's *Big Magic* workshop that inspired me to get started. I needed that final push - that inspiration. If I'd pushed myself to do it before, I just don't think I would have been ready. It's that subtle difference between pushing yourself over the line when the time is right vs pushing yourself to be ready.

Time takes its time

As well as the possibility that you might not be ready, it's also possible it's just not quite the right time. I'm a great believer that time takes its time - and by that, I mean we don't always get to simply decide when we want things to happen. If you think that might be the case, acknowledging this and finding a way to still take some small action without the pressure of achieving results, at least for now, is a good way to go.

Is it what you want, what you really, really (really) want?

But there's another reason that you might not be taking action, and that's because it's not something you really, really (really) want. You might be trying to make a change because you think you should or to meet someone else's agenda. We often don't even realise that's what we're doing until we explore it a bit more deeply.

Getting in touch with what you really want is actually quite hard. We're so accustomed to being told what we want that we barely know what we want for ourselves. This can be half the work, and actually, in my experience of coaching, is often most of the work.

So be as honest as you can (it took me years – and is still a work in progress – to connect to what I really want). Check with yourself and be kind if you realise that what you're trying to achieve isn't something you really want, right now – of course this can change.

The exercises in this book are designed to help you work through these things but this one can be hard to spot. Doing the exercises in the *Life Manifesto* section might be worth a try if you have any doubt.

Of course, if you're not taking action, you may just need some extra support in taking the first few steps and that's OK too. There is help out there, in many forms.

REVIEWING, REFLECTING AND LEARNING

Looking back; reviewing, reflecting and learning is really important, especially when you're trying something out. Taking the time to notice what you enjoyed, didn't like, etc., helps you to capture things it's sometimes easy to forget. You can then use this information to help decide inform your next, *What's next?*

I've included some exercises here to help you do just this.

You can also use this exercise to explore a topic more broadly before getting into the detail.

For example, if you're thinking of changing your career, you can review your current or previous jobs to surface what you enjoyed, found challenging, etc.

You can also use these exercises to review a particular period in your life where something happened/didn't happen, an event or the beginning/ending of something.

Reviewing, reflecting and learning

ENJOYED, NOTICED, LEARNED

First, think about the period of time, new activity or event you're going to review. If there's something in particular you're hoping to learn, for example, did something give you energy or not, add this into the prompt questions before you begin. Of course, once you get going, you can add in whatever you please.

Prompt: I enjoyed ... I noticed ... I learned ...

List: I recommend doing this exercise as a list. In a list, you repeat the prompt each time followed by your response. It doesn't matter if you repeat yourself, just keep the pen moving and something new will pop out.

Free-writing rules

- Set a timer for five minutes so you can let go into the journaling (you can always write more if you want to).
- Keep your pen moving (no editing or looking back) and follow your own emerging topic, even if it's about something else, it will still be important.
- If you get stuck, repeat the prompt or the last two words you wrote, if you feel resistance, annoyance or anything else, write about that.
- If you bump into difficult feelings, either write about them in detail (what does it feel like, where in your body can you feel it, what colour, texture, shape is it, etc.) or make a note to come back to it later when you have the support you need. Refer to the 'It's all about you' section for more.

General reflection questions

- What do you notice about what you wrote?
- Did you miss anything obvious?
- Does something particular stand out?
- How do you feel? Is your energy different after writing?
- Are there any words or phrases calling your attention? If so, make a note of them to use for onward prompts another time.
- Are there any beliefs that need to be checked or updated?

Specific reflection questions

- Was there anything you remembered that might have got lost?
- Can you get into even more detail?

NOTES

Good luck!

I hope that you're feeling confident to go about making some change in your life and taking back a bit of control.

As I've mentioned, this isn't a simple step by step process though I've laid it out as such for simplicity. Our behaviour, our blocks, our lives, they're all complex. So be kind to yourself and be patient.

It's my hope that you'll find that journaling can help you get pretty far if you give yourself the space and time to do it, but if you need some additional help, please ask for it.

Good luck to you and I'd love to hear about how you've used these exercises, or journaling in general to manage and change your life.

CP

NOTES

EXAMPLES

I encourage you to be free to write whatever comes for you if you can, rather than be influenced by what I wrote. But I appreciate sometimes you just want the comfort of seeing what someone else has done.

If you need them, here are my examples (just an opening sentence or two) followed by a reflection for each exercise. I free-wrote them so hopefully this will encourage you to do the same. What I got out of those first few sentences may or may not have hit the target but it's OK because the exercises can be repeated and your response will be different each time.

These are just the first few sentences I wrote in response to the prompts, so don't use this as a guide for quantity.

Write as much as you can in the allotted time; generally, five minutes and keep going even if you feel like you've initially concluded something.

Life Manifesto

HOSTILE OR FRIENDLY UNIVERSE?

Prompt: The Universe is …

Example

The Universe is immense and awe-inspiring. It simply can't be personal. So, it's neither hostile nor friendly. It just is. That leaves it up to me, to make my own meaning. I like Einstein's idea that our job is just to leave the place - the world - in good order for the next people that follow us. Simple.

My reflection:

This is something I've learned a lot about and realised recently. That meaning is up to me to develop. I find this quite an inspiring idea and it's nice to see it captured here.

It also tells me that I quote and talk about Einstein a lot, but he was brilliant.

Life Manifesto

WHAT DO YOU EXPECT?

Prompt: In life, I expect …

Example

In life I expect that I won't get much. I also expect that I'll get everything. I think I flit. I've convinced myself that I can live on the bare minimum in order to make myself more self-sufficient, but it's become something I identify with and I want that to change.

My reflection

There are a few reflections here. It was liberating to accept that I flit, as I do with a lot of things. I can fall foul of the urge to have every aspect of myself pinned down, as we all can.

It was noticeable but not surprising that I went straight to money. The context of the quote "When you stop expecting less, you get more" was about money, but it's not just that. I tend to always think of that first because it's related to survival. Something else to reflect on, am I still in 'survival mode?' I will note this and use it as an onward prompt, something I recommend you do every time you write.

Life Manifesto

WHAT DO YOU BELIEVE ABOUT LIFE?

Prompt: I believe that life is …

Example

I believe that life is just doing its thing. Life is what you make it. There are two worlds, we can make it a heaven or a hell - someone famous said that but I think it's true. I think what we expect along with what we feel is our story acts as a filter to what life has to offer, which is terrifying and liberating at the same time because it means I can choose a different filter.

My reflection

It doesn't take long for me to get philosophical and what I've written doesn't surprise me at all. I know this is what I think. But it's interesting that in the moment when I wrote it, it sort of struck me again, just how powerful this truth is, for me and how exciting it is to know that we can choose something different for ourselves.

Life Manifesto

WHAT DO YOU DESERVE?

Prompt: In life, I deserve …

Example

In life I deserve what I work for. I think. I deserve a chance. I deserve to be rewarded for what I do. I deserve what everyone else deserves, I haven't always thought that, what a shame.

My reflection

This feels a little unsure and it's true. It's not something I've not delved into directly. It's worth some more investigation. It's also good to acknowledge that yes, it is a shame that I didn't always feel this in my life. I can't change the past but I can change the future.

Life Manifesto

WHOSE AGENDA ARE YOU ON?

Prompt: I'm on …

Example

I'm on my agenda. At last! The trouble is that I sometimes forget there are still old messages guiding my agenda. So, in some ways it's not true that it's my own — what even is my own? That doesn't come from someone else?

My reflection

No matter how many times I ask myself this question, it amazes that I always come up with a different answer. Sometimes I'm super-clear, others, like this piece, it feels like there are still questions.

Whose agenda we're on is multi-layered and complex. The most important thing for me is that I finally feel like I'm on my own agenda, and that's a good start. But it reminds me to keep asking the question and peeling back the layers.

Life Manifesto

DEFINITION OF SUCCESS

Prompt: Success is…'

Example

Success is really simple for me. I just want a garden to sit in. To take my book and sit in the warm sunshine with a drink and nothing else to do.

My reflection

There is obviously a lot more to this, but the opening sentence captures something I'm really craving right now. It's a bout space, peace and nature; all things that I need more of – things we all need more of.

Life Manifesto

PERMISSION

Prompt: I give myself permission to …

Example

I give myself permission to be a writer, to be creative, to be organised and to like tidying and to be all these things, and more, at the same time.

My reflection

This has been a big theme for me. I struggle to allow myself to be things that are seemingly incongruent. For example, writing and tidying. I've long believed that writers are artistic and organic and take their time to 'birth' their work. I, on the other hand am very task-focused and a bit too organised.

Firstly, whilst writers as I've described do exist, there are many different kinds of writers. Also, who says I can't be organised and a writer. It's in questioning these long-held beliefs and societal tropes that keep us in our perceived place. Also, I could simply look at editing as 'tidying,' which is essentially what it is.

Life Manifesto

THANKS (GRATITUDE)

Prompt: Dear [Name], thank you …

Here I've chosen my friend Jason to write to.

Example

Dear Jason, thank you for being my friend. You always say this in greeting cards, but I feel like the lucky one. You see me more than almost anyone I've ever known, it's a great privilege to experience this.

My reflection

I've written about and to my friends before, so this was easy to conjure. It reminded me that my friend Jason really does see me and I can't be reminded of this often enough.

Warming Up

BRAIN DUMP

Prompt: What's currently happening is …

Example

What's currently happening is that I'm sitting at my desk writing the final touches to the book as it goes into the template for (self) publishing. I missed a couple of prompts when I was writing it and this is one of them. I'm listening to 'The times they are a changing,' by The Brothers and Sisters (a Dylan covers album).

My reflection

As I wrote this, I felt a little tingle of pride. I've done it, I've (pretty much) finished this book. It took a while and it was hard at times, but I've done it. I've chosen to see meaning in the Dylan song. The times are indeed 'a' changing' as I step into myself more and more and take my space in the world, something I've avoided until now.

I wrote to this prompt from a good place, but often, when we're a bit overloaded this can be a great exercise to clear some space and see what's going on.

Warming Up

SIX SENSES

Prompt: I feel ... I see ... I hear ... I smell ... I taste ... I sense ...

Example

I feel a bit strange, like I have a mental health virus, I see my computer screen, always there, always passive and waiting for me to bring it to life. I hear Dylan covers playing – my current obsession, I smell the absence of my next coffee, I taste traces of the last one. I sense that I am in a strange place, a place of change, the uncomfortable bit.

My reflection

Even when I know things are amiss, I find it's worth reminding myself so I can be a bit gentle with myself. It also reminds me – in writing about a 'virus' - that what I'm experiencing could be physical. It's so easy to feel something and backfill it with thoughts, something I'm able to stop myself doing more and more.

My comment about my computer waiting for me to bring it to life feels like something important. Is it waiting for me or is it the other way around?

I quite enjoy my writing when it's a little darker. I get a bit poetic and whilst I'm no poet, I do quite enjoy reading back what I've written and perhaps one day I will write some poetry.

Warming Up

BIBLE DIP (it doesn't have to be a bible)

Prompt: I've just done a bible dip in a book about nature and my finger landed on 'half-horse.'

Example

Half-horse is a very sweet horse. He spends all his time in his stable, only his head poking out, and this is why people call him 'half-horse.' He's quite content looking out and seeing the world and isn't concerned about being enclosed because he only looks out, never back.

My reflection

As I've done here, free-writing may become fictional. Even if it does, there is always information in what you've written. What can you relate to in the characters you've created, the situations they're in?

I think that Half-horse is a very content horse that has a small life where things are simple. I felt very peaceful writing and reading this back, something I strive for in my own life. The last line is very poignant for me right now as I'm focusing on looking forward. I'm finished with looking back.

People sometimes use free-writing to generate ideas for their creative writing. I'm wondering, having just written about 'half-horse' whether this story has legs... I couldn't resist the pun. Anyway, it doesn't matter, it got me writing - job done.

What's happening now?

INTO THE WEEDS

Prompt: What's happening is …

Example

Here, I'm going to think about how I've not been journaling as much lately:

"What's happening is I'm not doing much journaling. I write for work and I do enjoy it, but it always has a purpose in mind … I miss just scribbling away …" All that said, I tend to journal 'medicinally,' when there's a problem. Of late there has been less need for that. Hooray.

My reflection

The most significant reflection here is that it reminded me I tend to only journal when I'm troubled about something. It's great that I clearly wasn't when I wrote this, but it's a good reminder that journaling can be about good things too.

What's happening now?

FROM THE MOUNTAIN TOP

Prompt: From up here …

Example

From up here, I can see myself, head down looking only at work, work, work. I love my work, but I'm not looking up and around me to see what else life has to offer.

My reflection

It's pretty immediate that I can see a problem. I know I'm not focusing on things other than work – which of course I love – as much as I should.

Whilst I did know it, the extra perspective I got from looking from above was impactful. I saw the wider context; life going on around me whilst my head is down. Something to explore more.

What's happening now?

NEWSPAPER ARTICLE

Prompt: Pick a title for your article, for example: 'Woman struggles over difficult decision about which outfit fits 'smart/casual' for upcoming conference!' (this actually did happen to me recently – my solution? To take everything.)

Example

Here I used the above example of my attendance at a conference where the dress code was 'business casual.' Having not been to something in person for a while, this was causing me a little stress. So here it is. "Woman struggles over difficult decision about which outfit fits 'smart/casual' for upcoming conference."

"A middle-aged woman, invited to a conference recently had a difficult dilemma. Just what was 'business/casual?!' It was hard enough to interpret in the 80s and 90s, but now that people are generally more casual in business, just what did this mean? She spoke to friends and colleagues and gathered as much information as possible."

My reflection

This helps me to set out the details of the situation I'm in. Immediately I'm reminded that this is just a social etiquette dilemma that I'm perhaps wasting too much time thinking about. When you carry on and get into the detail you can surface other insights and even ideas of how to deal with a situation. This actually also serves to remind me to have a sense of humour about some things in life, is it really that important?

Goals - Exploring

IF I LIVED FOREVER

Prompt: If I lived forever…

Example

If I lived forever, I'd make a list of everything I always wanted to try and tick them off one by one, no matter how long they took. I'd learn about the body so I could make my own decisions about what to put on it and in it …

My reflection

I know that my initial words are somewhat predictable, but when this exercise gets going is when it starts to get interesting. Even so, it shows immediately that there's something here about agency for me. I want to make more conscious decisions about how I live my life.

Goals – Exploring

ALTERNATIVE LIVES

Prompt: I am a …

(The guidance is to first thing of two or three. Mine were: A lady who lunches, a philosophy student sitting around chatting about ideas on a big fancy lawn (in front of a brownstone university). A writer working with a team on a sitcom or similar. For this example, I chose 'A lady who lunches.)

Example

"I am a lady who lunches. I can't get enough Champagne into my body soon enough so really, I'm a lady who prefers to breakfast than to lunch…"

My reflection

I really enjoyed leaning into this life of luxury and leisure. There were some, less appealing aspects of my 'lady who lunches' personality once I got stuck into the writing. For me, accepting the less pretty parts is just as important as the stuff I aspire to.

It also highlights my longing for the finer things which I can convince myself I can live happily without. Of course, I can live without them, but I shouldn't deny myself the desire.

Goals - Exploring

'WOULDN'T IT BE LOVELY'

Prompt: Wouldn't it be lovely…

Example

Wouldn't it be lovely if the sun would come out, wouldn't it be lovely if the world could heal itself … Wouldn't it be lovely if I could convince everyone to pick up a pen!

My reflection

I noticed that I initially went for external things, things I *should* be wishing for. Then, unsurprisingly my slight hint of world domination crept in.

This exercise gives me complete permission to think big which is one of the things I love about it. This kind of big ambition wouldn't come up in conversation and by writing it down, it becomes a possibility.

Goals – Clarifying

EXPLAIN YOURSELF

Prompt: I want to…

(Reminder that with this exercise you explain your goal to your chosen nan and/or child).

Example

Using this book as my goal I wrote to a young child, about 9 or 10 (we got into a bit of a dialogue on the page which I've decided to include in its entirety):

Me: "I'm going to write a book with writing exercises in it so that people can help themselves when they need help in their lives, if they don't have someone to hand."
Child: So, you're going to write a story?
Me: No, it's a self-help book.
Child: What's that?
Me: Well, it a book that helps people understand life and how to navigate it.
Child: What, like sailors?
Me: No, that's just an expression… Let me try again. So, life can be hard.
Child: Oh no!
Me: But it's OK. It can be hard but we can make it easier by dealing with things in certain ways.
Child: You mean, if I tidy my room, then I don't get told off?
Me: Kind of, yes. Imagine there was a book that had things like that in it, that would help you to know what to do, how to make decisions yourself."
Child: What do you mean 'make decisions?' I have to tidy my room.
Me: Maybe we can think of a better example. Let's say you have to decide between two toys you can buy. How do you decide?
Child: Easy, I pick my favourite.

Me: What if you don't know which your favourite is?

Child: I always know which my favourite is.

Me: Yes, of course you do, you're a child. That's it. When you get older, you forget those things. Other things make it hard to remember which your favourite is and this book will help people to remember.

Child: That sounds weird, how do you forget?

Me: Well, you have so many things you have to do as a grown up. I know you do too, but you don't have to decide. You often get told what to do don't you?

Child: Yes, but I don't like that. I want to do what I want.

Me: Yes, well it comes with a price.

Child: (looks confused)

Me: Anyway. It's annoying to be told what to do yes, but when you have to decide everything for yourself there's just so many things you think you should do, there's things you want to do, but there's things you must do, things you should do, the list goes on and on.

Child: Why don't you just do what you want?

Me: Good point.

Reflection

This tells me how hard it is to explain how we go from knowing exactly what we like, want to do, etc., as a child to being overwhelmed by expectations and pressures. What a great reminder this is of what this book is about. It's about remembering what you love and what you want, not finding it. This is something I've always believed, that we just need to come back to ourselves.

It also made me remember not to use corporate words like, 'navigate.' I really resisted that word when it first worked its way into day-to-day life and here, I'm using it with a child …

Goals – Clarifying

MANIFEST MEMOIR

Prompt: It's really happening…

Example

It's really happening, I've written the book. It's sitting on my desk and to see it and touch it is a thrill I could never have imagined … Not only that, people actually seem to want to buy it, lots of people!

My reflection

Journaling allows me to imagine and define success which, in my opinion, will help me to make things happen. Writing this stuff down is powerful and when I read it back, I can think, "Yes, why not!?" I feel excited, hopeful and motivated. All things that will help get this book finished.

Goals - Clarifying

30 WORDS

Prompt: Start with one of the words or phrases you've picked out. I picked out 'amazing, tools, life, easier, enjoyable, share and help.'

Example

Life is hard. I want people to make theirs easier, and more enjoyable. I have these amazing tools and I want to share them so people can help themselves.

My reflection

I had to do a quick edit to get it to less than 30 words. It made my goal more succinct and clearer. It's a really good exercise to get something down to its core. This sentence really sums up how I feel and what I want to achieve.

Reviewing, reflecting and learning

ENJOYED, NOTICED, LEARNED

Prompt: I enjoyed, noticed, learned ...

Example

(Thinking about lockdown): *'I enjoyed the simplicity; I enjoyed the quiet...' 'I missed very little...' I learned that a smaller, simpler life is actually much richer than one full of activities...'*

My reflection

Despite the brevity (remember, I'm only sharing an opening sentence or two), it really does sum up what I learned from that time and I need constantly reminding that a simpler life can be richer.

10. RESOURCES

It's impossible to look back and say exactly what helped and at what point. A grain of a thought here can turn into a fully formed 'aha moment' there without us even knowing. All that said, there are many resources that have contributed to my experience and definitely to the development of these exercises. So here goes:

Firstly, here's my website where you can find information on coaching, workshops (public and corporate) and courses. www.clairepearce.uk.

Mental health and wellbeing

MIND

I've visited MIND's website many times, both in and out of a work context. They have fantastic resources and support available.

https://www.mind.org.uk/

Mental Health First Aid England

I completed the Mental Health First Aider training in January 2022. I'd thoroughly recommend it. I knew quite a lot and you will too; things I'd picked up in my work, volunteering, from my own personal experience and those around me.

What this training does is bring it all together and fill in the gaps. I now feel much more confident that I would be doing the right thing should I need to help someone, and I also have a broader perspective on all thing's mental health. I really recommend the training just for life in general, and especially if you're in a position where you're supporting people in any way. Like MIND, they have loads of really good resources, so take a few minutes to check out their website.

https://mhfaengland.org/

Books – self-development

We've all read lots of books and I especially enjoy non-fiction including business and self-help books. I could fill a book with reviews, but here I'm just going to list a few that I would heartily recommend.

Change your questions, Change your life – Marilee Adams

As mentioned, this was a bit of a difficult read as it's written as a fable and I'm not a fan of fables. BUT the messages and advice are undeniably useful and this book has genuinely changed the way I think. Barely a day goes by when I don't ask myself, "Is this the right question?"

Bird by Bird – Anne Lamott

Whether you're a writer or not, Anne's lovely writing style and simple messages are relevant, whatever you do. It's a quick, light read and will leave you with lots of good, nourishing advice for writing, for life.

Daring Greatly – Brené Brown

Obviously, I had to include this. Brené breaks open our thinking about human behaviour with research, not fluff. I personally would recommend the TED talk she gave that shot her to fame, *The power of vulnerability*.

Learned Optimism – Martin Seligman

A lot of self-help books regurgitate this source material. It's based on research and Martin Seligman was one of the founders of Positive Psychology. It helps those of us more inclined to pessimism to learn to have a different mindset. I wrote a very brief summary of it in my blog: *Pessimism and Mars Bars* on my website under 'blog.'

Awareness – Anthony DeMello

The answer is always, 'awareness.' This book hit me like a tonne of bricks when I read it. Anthony DeMello was a Jesuit Priest and psychotherapist and his book is full of wisdom from multiple disciplines and well worth a read.

Journal to the Self – Kathleen Adams

I did course based on this book at *City Lit* in London. It was the second journaling workshop I attended. This is the book I'd probably recommend above all others for the range of exercises and just general readability.

Writing for self-discovery – Myra Schneider & John Killick

Another book with great journaling exercises.

At a Journaling Workshop – Ira Progoff

A lot of the exercises in journaling books have their roots in Ira Progoff's approaches, so he needs a mention. He worked with Jung and developed a programme of deep exploration. I haven't yet made it through the book (it's pretty hefty) but there's some great stuff in it. I have a plan to write a summary of it … one day.

The Artist's Way by Julia Cameron (she of Morning Pages).

Julia deserves a mention simply based on how amazingly successful her book is and continues to be. This book is more about unleashing creativity than straight self-discovery. It inspired some great exercises for me and is definitely a good one for self-exploration, whatever your intention.

The School of Life

I love the *School of Life* and their offerings. Founded by Alain De Botton, the school shares ancient philosophical wisdom and makes it relevant for modern life. I like to follow them on Twitter but they have a tonne of resources and of course, books. They also run workshops and courses.

Writing courses/retreats

Fire in the head retreat – Roselle Angwin
https://roselle-angwin.co.uk/author/roselleangwin/

Freefall – writing as creative therapy course – Gestalt Centre (Where it all began for me)
https://gestaltcentre.org.uk/course/writing-as-creative-therapy/

REFERENCES

Einstein quote: https://www.goodreads.com/quotes/429690-the-most-important-decision-we-make-is-whether-we-believe

Elizabeth Gilbert quote: https://www.oprah.com/own-super-soul-sunday/elizabeth-gilbert-give-yourself-permission-to-honor-your-life-video

Confucius quote: https://www.brainyquote.com/quotes/confucius_104563?src=t_life

Curtis Tyrone Jones quote: https://www.goodreads.com/quotes/tag/visualizing

Maya Angelou quote: https://philosiblog.com/2013/11/01/success-is-liking-yourself-liking-what-you-do-and-liking-how-you-do-it/

Unbelievable: https://www.imdb.com/title/tt7909970/

Thomas Edison quote: https://www.goodreads.com/quotes/97717-when-you-have-exhausted-all-possibilities-remember-this---you

Marcel Proust quote: https://www.goodreads.com/quotes/7810-let-us-be-grateful-to-the-people-who-make-us

THANK YOU

I'd never pictured writing this part of my book. I used to have a picture of the back cover with my photo and some squiggly text – vision board style, but I never thought about what lay beneath, mainly because, at that stage, I didn't know what the book would be about.

In the same way that I can't say specifically what helped and at what time on my journey, it's the same with people. Foes as well as friends have contributed to the motivation and completion of this book.

But, like free-writing and journaling, which I know helped, I can say that having the wonderful people in my life I'm lucky enough to call my friends, has definitely contributed to me being me and getting this book written. You know who you are. Thank you.

I'd also like to thank those who directly helped me to develop, shape and edit this book: Annie, Kirsty, Katie and Nic. Also, to those who attended the very first, *Coach yourself with a Pen* course.

Finally, I'd like to thank my ex-therapist Angelika, for encouraging me to do my very first free-writing course, which, for the record, I was very resistant about. Thank you.

ABOUT ME - CP

I've been using creative writing and journaling techniques for many years now. As someone who is a bit, 'jack of all trades,' the fact that writing and journaling has prevailed is evidence that it is indeed, 'my thing' – something I could only dream about having in my old corporate life.

As I've probably mentioned, I want you to have an easier, more enjoyable life and I'm pretty evangelical about how journaling can help to make this a reality. I run regular Creative group journaling sessions, courses and coaching sessions on journaling, self-discovery and other self-help topics.

I'm also love to get involved with developmental editing on non-fiction books.

Printed in Great Britain
by Amazon

25180650R10096